TOLSTOY ON SHAKESPEARE,
(A critical Essay on Shakespeare)
By Leo Tolstoy.

CONTENTS

PART I

PAGE TOLSTOY ON SHAKESPEARE 1

PART II

APPENDIX

I. SHAKESPEARE'S ATTITUDE TOWARD THE WORKING CLASSES, BY ERNEST CROSBY, 127

II. LETTER FROM MR. G. BERNARD SHAW, 166

PART I

TOLSTOY ON SHAKESPEARE

I

Mr. Crosby's article[1] on Shakespeare's attitude toward the working classes suggested to me the idea of also expressing my own long-established opinion about the works of Shakespeare, in direct opposition, as it is, to that established in all the whole European world. Calling to mind all the struggle of doubt and self-deceit,--efforts to attune myself to Shakespeare--which I went through owing to my complete disagreement with this universal adulation, and, presuming that many have experienced and are experiencing the same, I think that it may not be unprofitable to express definitely and frankly this view of mine, opposed to that of the majority, and the more so as the conclusions to which I came, when examining the causes of my disagreement with the universally established opinion, are, it seems to me, not without interest and significance.

My disagreement with the established opinion about Shakespeare is not the result of an accidental frame of mind, nor of a light-minded attitude toward the matter, but is the outcome of many years' repeated and insistent endeavors to harmonize my own views of Shakespeare with those established amongst all civilized men of the Christian world.

I remember the astonishment I felt when I first read Shakespeare. I expected to receive a powerful esthetic pleasure, but having read, one after the other, works regarded as his best: "King Lear," "Romeo and Juliet," "Hamlet" and "Macbeth," not only did I feel no delight, but I felt an irresistible repulsion and tedium, and doubted as to whether I was senseless in feeling works regarded as the summit of perfection by the whole of the civilized world to be trivial and positively bad, or whether the significance which this civilized world attributes to the works of Shakespeare was itself senseless. My consternation was increased by the fact that I always keenly felt the beauties of poetry in every form; then why should artistic works recognized by the whole world as those of a genius,--the works of Shakespeare,--not only fail to please me, but be disagreeable to me? For a long time I could not believe in myself, and during fifty years, in order to test myself, I several times recommenced reading Shakespeare in every possible form, in Russian, in English, in German and in Schlegel's translation, as I was advised. Several times I read the dramas and the comedies and historical plays, and I invariably underwent the same feelings: repulsion, weariness, and bewilderment. At the present time, before writing this preface, being desirous once more to test myself, I have, as an old man of seventy-five, again read the whole of Shakespeare, including the historical plays, the "Henrys," "Troilus and Cressida," the "Tempest," "Cymbeline," and I have felt, with even greater force, the same feelings,--this time, however, not of bewilderment, but of firm, indubitable conviction that the unquestionable glory of a great genius which Shakespeare enjoys, and which compels writers of our time to imitate him and readers and spectators to discover in him non-existent merits,--thereby distorting their esthetic and ethical understanding,--is a great evil, as is every untruth.

Altho I know that the majority of people so firmly believe in the greatness of Shakespeare that in reading this judgment of mine they will not admit even the possibility of its justice, and will not give it the slightest attention, nevertheless I will endeavor, as well as I can, to show why I believe that Shakespeare can not be recognized either as a great genius, or even as an average author.

For illustration of my purpose I will take one of Shakespeare's most extolled dramas, "King Lear," in the enthusiastic praise of which, the majority of critics agree.

"The tragedy of Lear is deservedly celebrated among the dramas of Shakespeare," says Dr. Johnson. "There is perhaps no play which keeps the attention so strongly fixed, which so much agitates our passions, and interests our curiosity."

"We wish that we could pass this play over and say nothing about it," says Hazlitt, "all that we can say must fall far short of the subject, or even of what we ourselves conceive of it. To attempt to give a description of the play itself, or of its effects upon the mind, is mere impertinence; yet we must say something. It is, then, the best of Shakespeare's plays, for it is the one in which he was the most in earnest."

"If the originality of invention did not so much stamp almost every play of Shakespeare," says Hallam, "that to name one as the most original seems a disparagement to others, we might say that this great prerogative of genius, was exercised above all in 'Lear.' It diverges more from the model of regular tragedy than 'Macbeth,' or 'Othello,' and even more than 'Hamlet,' but the fable is better constructed than in the last of these and it displays full as much of the almost superhuman inspiration of the poet as the other two."

"'King Lear' may be recognized as the perfect model of the dramatic art of the whole world," says Shelley.

"I am not minded to say much of Shakespeare's Arthur," says Swinburne. "There are one or two figures in the world of his work of which there are no words that would be fit or good to say. Another of these is Cordelia. The place they have in our lives and thoughts is not one for talk. The niche set apart for them to inhabit in our secret hearts is not penetrable by the lights and noises of common day. There are chapels in the cathedrals of man's highest art, as in that of his inmost life, not made to be set open to the eyes and feet of the world. Love, and Death, and Memory, keep charge for us in silence of some beloved names. It is the crowning glory of genius, the final miracle and transcendent gift of poetry, that it can add to the number of these and engrave on the very heart of our remembrance fresh names and memories of its own creation."

"Lear is the occasion for Cordelia," says Victor Hugo. "Maternity of the daughter toward the father; profound subject; maternity venerable among all other maternities, so admirably rendered by the legend of that Roman girl, who, in the depths of a prison, nurses her old father. The young breast near the white beard! There is not a spectacle more holy. This filial breast is Cordelia. Once this figure dreamed of and found, Shakespeare created his drama.... Shakespeare, carrying Cordelia in his thoughts, created that tragedy like a god who, having an aurora to put forward, makes a world expressly for it."

"In 'King Lear,' Shakespeare's vision sounded the abyss of horror to its very depths, and his spirit showed neither fear, nor giddiness, nor faintness, at the sight," says Brandes. "On the threshold of this work, a feeling of awe comes over one, as on the threshold of the Sistine Chapel, with its ceiling of frescoes by Michael Angelo,--only that the suffering here is far more intense, the wail wilder, and the harmonies of beauty more definitely shattered by the discords of despair."

Such are the judgments of the critics about this drama, and therefore I believe I am not wrong in selecting it as a type of Shakespeare's best.

As impartially as possible, I will endeavor to describe the contents of the drama, and then to show why it is not that acme of perfection it is represented to be by critics, but is something quite different.

II

The drama of "Lear" begins with a scene giving the conversation between two courtiers, Kent and Gloucester. Kent, pointing to a young man present, asks Gloucester whether that is not his son.

Gloucester says that he has often blushed to acknowledge the young man as his son, but has now ceased doing so. Kent says he "can not conceive him." Then Gloucester in the presence of this son of his says: "The fellow's mother could, and grew round-wombed, and had a son for her cradle ere she had a husband for her bed." "I have another, a legitimate son," continues Gloucester, "but altho this one came into the world before he was sent for, his mother was fair and there was good sport at his making, and therefore I acknowledge this one also."

Such is the introduction. Not to mention the coarseness of these words of Gloucester, they are, farther, out of place in the mouth of a person intended to represent a noble character. One can not agree with the opinion of some critics that these words are given to Gloucester in order to show the contempt for his illegitimacy from which Edmund suffers. Were this so, it would first have been unnecessary to make the father express the contempt felt by men in general, and, secondly, Edmund, in his monolog about the injustice of those who despise him for his birth, would have mentioned such words from his father. But this is not so, and therefore these words of Gloucester at the very beginning of the piece, were merely intended as a communication to the public--in a humorous form--of the fact that Gloucester has a legitimate son and an illegitimate one.

After this, trumpets are blown, and King Lear enters with his daughters and sons-in-law, and utters a speech to the effect that, owing to old age, he wishes to retire from the cares of business and divide his kingdom between his daughters. In order to know how much he should give to each daughter, he announces that to the one who says she loves him most he will give most. The eldest daughter, Goneril, says that words can not express the extent of her love, that she loves her father more than eyesight, space, and liberty, loves him so much that it "makes her breath poor." King Lear immediately allots his daughter on the map, her portion of fields, woods, rivers, and meadows, and asks the same question of the second daughter. The second daughter, Regan, says that her sister has correctly expressed her own feelings, only not strongly enough. She, Regan, loves her father so much that everything is abhorrent to her except his love. The king rewards this daughter, also, and then asks his youngest, the favorite, in whom, according to his expression, are "interess'd the vines of France and the milk of Burgundy," that is, whose hand is being claimed by the King of France and the Duke of Burgundy,--he asks Cordelia how she loves him. Cordelia, who personifies all the virtues, as the eldest two all the vices, says, quite out of place, as if on purpose to irritate her father, that altho she loves and honors him, and is grateful to him, yet if she marries, all her love will not belong to her father, but she will also love her husband.

Hearing these words, the King loses his temper, and curses this favorite daughter with the most dreadful and strange maledictions, saying, for instance, that he will henceforth love his daughter as little as he loves the man who devours his own children.

"The barbarous Scythian, Or he that makes his generation messes To gorge his appetite, shall to my bosom Be as well neighbour'd, pitied, and relieved. As thou, my sometime daughter."

The courtier, Kent, defends Cordelia, and desiring to appease the King, rebukes him for his injustice, and says reasonable things about the evil of flattery. Lear, unmoved by Kent, banishes him under pain of death, and calling to him Cordelia's two suitors, the Duke of Burgundy and the King of France, proposes to them in turn to take Cordelia without dowry. The Duke of Burgundy frankly says that without dowry he will not take Cordelia, but the King of France takes her without dowry and leads her away. After this, the elder sisters, there and then entering into conversation, prepare to injure their father who had endowed them. Thus ends the first scene.

Not to mention the pompous, characterless language of King Lear, the same in which all Shakespeare's Kings speak, the reader, or spectator, can not conceive that a King, however old and stupid he may be, could believe the words of the vicious daughters, with whom he had passed his whole life, and not believe his favorite daughter, but curse and banish her; and therefore the spectator, or reader, can not share the feelings of the persons participating in this unnatural scene.

The second scene opens with Edmund, Gloucester's illegitimate son, soliloquizing on the injustice of men, who concede rights and respect to the legitimate son, but deprive the illegitimate son of them, and he determines to ruin Edgar, and to usurp his place. For this purpose, he forges a letter to himself as from Edgar, in which the latter expresses a desire to murder his father. Awaiting his father's approach, Edmund, as if against his will, shows him this letter, and the father immediately believes that his son Edgar, whom he tenderly loves, desires to kill him. The father goes away, Edgar enters and Edmund persuades him that his father for some reason desires to kill him. Edgar immediately believes this and flees from his parent.

The relations between Gloucester and his two sons, and the feelings of these characters are as unnatural as Lear's relation to his daughters, or even more so, and therefore it is still more difficult for the spectator to transport himself into the mental condition of Gloucester and his sons and sympathize with them, than it is to do so into that of Lear and his daughters.

In the fourth scene, the banished Kent, so disguised that Lear does not recognize him, presents himself to Lear, who is already staying with Goneril. Lear asks who he is, to which Kent answers, one doesn't know why, in a tone quite inappropriate to his position: "A very honest-hearted fellow and as poor as the King."--"If thou be as poor for a subject as he is for a King, thou art poor enough--How old art thou?" asks the King. "Not so young, Sir, to love a woman, *etc.*, nor so old to dote on her." To this the King says, "If I like thee no worse after dinner, I will not part from thee yet."

These speeches follow neither from Lear's position, nor his relation to Kent, but are put into the mouths of Lear and Kent, evidently because the author regards them as witty and amusing.

Goneril's steward appears, and behaves rudely to Lear, for which Kent knocks him down. The King, still not recognizing Kent, gives him money for this and takes him into his service. After this appears the fool, and thereupon begins a prolonged conversation between the fool and the King, utterly unsuited to the position and serving no purpose. Thus, for instance, the fool says, "Give me an egg and I'll give thee two crowns." The King asks, "What crowns shall they be?"--"Why," says the fool, "after I have cut the egg i' the middle, and eat up the meat, the two crowns of the egg. When thou clovest thy crown i' the middle, and gavest away both parts, thou borest thine ass on thy back o'er the dirt: thou hadst little wit in thy bald crown when thou gavest thy golden one away. If I speak like myself in this, let him be whipp'd that first finds it so."

In this manner lengthy conversations go on calling forth in the spectator or reader that wearisome uneasiness which one experiences when listening to jokes which are not witty.

This conversation was interrupted by the approach of Goneril. She demands of her father that he should diminish his retinue; that he should be satisfied with fifty courtiers instead of a hundred. At this suggestion, Lear gets into a strange and unnatural rage, and asks:

"Doth any here know me? This is not Lear: Does Lear walk thus? speak thus? Where are his eyes? Either his notion weakens, his discernings Are lethargied. Ha! 'tis not so. Who is it that can tell me who I am?"

And so forth.

While this goes on the fool does not cease to interpolate his humorless jokes. Goneril's husband then enters and wishes to appease Lear, but Lear curses Goneril, invoking for her either sterility or the birth of such an infant-monster as would return laughter and contempt for her motherly cares, and would thus show her all the horror and pain caused by a child's ingratitude.

These words which express a genuine feeling, might have been touching had they stood alone. But they are lost among long and high-flown speeches, which Lear keeps incessantly uttering quite inappropriately. He either invokes "blasts and fogs" upon the head of his daughter, or desires his curse to "pierce every sense about her," or else appealing to his own eyes, says that should they weep, he will pluck them out and "cast them with the waters that they lose to temper clay." And so on.

After this, Lear sends Kent, whom he still fails to recognize, to his other daughter, and notwithstanding the despair he has just manifested, he talks with the fool, and elicits his jokes. The jokes continue to be mirthless and besides creating an unpleasant feeling, similar to shame, the usual effect of unsuccessful witticisms, they are also so drawn out as to be positively dull. Thus the fool asks the King whether he can tell why one's nose stands in the middle of one's face? Lear says he can not.--

"Why, to keep one's eyes of either side 's nose, that what a man can not smell out, he may spy out."

"Canst tell how an oyster makes his shell?"

"No."

"Nor I either; but I can tell why a snail has a house."

"Why?"

"Why, to put his head in; not to give it away to his daughters and leave his horns without a case."

"----Be my horses ready?"

"Thy asses are gone about 'em. The reason why the seven stars are no more than seven is a pretty reason."

"Because they are not eight?"

"Yes, indeed: thou would'st make a good fool."

And so on.

After this lengthy scene, a gentleman enters and announces that the horses are ready. The fool says:

"She that's a maid now, and laughs at my departure, Shall not be a maid long, unless things be cut shorter."

The second part of the first scene of the second act begins by the villain Edmund persuading his brother, when their father enters, to pretend that they are fighting with their swords. Edgar consents, altho it is utterly incomprehensible why he should do so. The father finds them fighting. Edgar flies and Edmund scratches his arm to draw blood and persuades his father that Edgar was working charms for the purpose of killing his father and had desired Edmund to help him, but that he, Edmund, had refused and that then Edgar flew at him and wounded his arm. Gloucester believes everything, curses Edgar and transfers all the rights of the elder and legitimate son to the illegitimate Edmund. The Duke, hearing of this, also rewards Edmund.

In the second scene, in front of Gloucester's palace, Lear's new servant, Kent, still unrecognized by Lear, without any reason, begins to abuse Oswald, Goneril's steward, calling him,--"A knave, a rascal, an eater of broken meats; a base, proud, shallow, beggarly, three-suited, hundred-pound, filthy, worsted-stocking knave;--the son and heir of a mongrel bitch." And so on. Then drawing his sword, he demands that Oswald should fight with him, saying that he will make a "sop o' the moonshine" of him,--words which no commentators can explain. When he is stopped, he continues to give vent to the strangest abuse, saying that a tailor made Oswald, as "a stone-cutter or a painter could not have made him so ill, tho they had been but two hours o' the trade!" He further says that, if only leave be given him, he will "tread this unbolted villain into mortar and daub the wall of a jakes with him."

Thus Kent, whom nobody recognizes, altho both the King and the Duke of Cornwall, as well as Gloucester who is present, ought to know him well, continues to brawl, in the character of Lear's new servant, until he is taken and put in the stocks.

The third scene takes place on a heath. Edgar, flying from the persecutions of his father, hides in a wood and tells the public what kind of lunatics exist there--beggars who go about naked, thrust wooden pricks and pins into their flesh, scream with wild voices and enforce charity, and says that he wishes to simulate such a lunatic in order to save himself from persecution. Having communicated this to the public, he retires.

The fourth scene is again before Gloucester's castle. Enter Lear and the fool. Lear sees Kent in the stocks, and, still not recognizing him, is inflamed with rage against those who dared so to insult his messenger, and calls for the Duke and Regan. The fool goes on with his jokes.

Lear with difficulty restrains his ire. Enter the Duke and Regan. Lear complains of Goneril but Regan justifies her sister. Lear curses Goneril, and, when Regan tells him he had better return to her sister, he is indignant and says: "Ask her forgiveness?" and falls down on his knees demonstrating how indecent it would be if he were abjectly to beg food and clothing as charity from his own daughter, and he curses Goneril with the strangest curses and asks who put his servant in the stocks. Before Regan can answer, Goneril arrives. Lear becomes yet more exasperated and again curses Goneril, but when he is told that it was the Duke himself who ordered the stocks, he does not say anything, because, at this moment, Regan tells him that she can not receive him now and that he had best return to Goneril, and that in a month's time she herself will receive him, with, however, not a hundred but fifty servants. Lear again curses Goneril and does not want to go to her, continuing to hope that Regan will accept him with the whole hundred servants. But Regan says she will receive him only with twenty-five and then Lear makes up his mind to go back to Goneril who admits fifty. But when Goneril says that even twenty-five are too many, Lear pours forth a long argument about the superfluous and the needful being relative and says that if man is not allowed more than he needs, he is not to be distinguished from a beast. Lear, or rather the actor who plays Lear's part, adds that there is no need for a lady's finery, which does not keep her warm. After this he flies into a mad fury and says that to take vengeance on his daughters he will do something dreadful but that he will not weep, and so he departs. A storm begins.

Such is the second act, full of unnatural events, and yet more unnatural speeches, not flowing from the position of the characters,--and finishing with a scene between Lear and his daughters which might have been powerful if it had not been permeated with the most absurdly foolish, unnatural speeches--which, moreover, have no relation to the subject,--put into the mouth of Lear. Lear's vacillations between pride, anger, and the hope of his daughters' giving in, would be exceedingly touching if it were not spoilt by the verbose absurdities to which he gives vent, about being ready to divorce himself from Regan's dead mother, should Regan not be glad to receive him,--or about his calling down "fen suck'd frogs" which he invokes, upon the head of his daughter, or about the heavens being obliged to patronize old people because they themselves are old.

The third act begins with thunder, lightning, a storm of some special kind such as, according to the words of the characters in the piece, had never before taken place. On the heath, a gentleman tells Kent that Lear, banished by his daughters from their homes, is running about the heath alone, tearing his hair and throwing it to the wind, and that none but the fool is with him. In return Kent tells the gentleman that the dukes have quarrelled, and that the French army has landed at Dover, and, having communicated this intelligence, he dispatches the gentleman to Dover to meet Cordelia.

The second scene of the third act also takes place on the heath, but in another part of it. Lear walks about the heath and says words which are meant to express his despair: he desires that the winds should blow so hard that they should crack their cheeks and that the rain should flood everything, that lightning should singe his white head, and the thunder flatten the world and destroy all germens "that make ungrateful man!" The fool keeps uttering still more senseless words. Enter Kent. Lear says that for some reason during this storm all criminals shall be found out and convicted. Kent, still unrecognized by Lear, endeavors to persuade him to take refuge in a hovel. At this point the fool pronounces a prophecy in no wise related to the situation and they all depart.

The third scene is again transferred to Gloucester's castle. Gloucester tells Edmund that the French King has already landed with his troops, and intends to help Lear. Learning this, Edmund decides to accuse his father of treason in order that he may get his heritage.

The fourth scene is again on the heath in front of the hovel. Kent invites Lear into the hovel, but Lear answers that he has no reason to shelter himself from the tempest, that he does not feel it, having a tempest in his mind, called forth by the ingratitude of his daughters, which extinguishes all else. This true feeling, expressed in simple words, might elicit sympathy, but amidst the incessant, pompous raving it escapes one and loses its significance.

The hovel into which Lear is led, turns out to be the same which Edgar has entered, disguised as a madman, *i.e.*, naked. Edgar comes out of the hovel, and, altho all have known him, no one recognizes him,--as no one recognizes Kent,--and Edgar, Lear, and the fool begin to say senseless things which continue with interruptions for many pages. In the middle of this scene, enter Gloucester, who also does not recognize either Kent or his son Edgar, and tells them how his son Edgar wanted to kill him.

This scene is again cut short by another in Gloucester's castle, during which Edmund betrays his father and the Duke promises to avenge himself on Gloucester. Then the scene shifts back to Lear. Kent, Edgar, Gloucester, Lear, and the fool are at a farm and talking. Edgar says: "Frateretto calls me, and tells me Nero is an angler in the lake of darkness...." The fool says: "Tell me whether a madman be a gentleman or a yeoman?" Lear, having lost his mind, says that the madman is a king. The fool says no, the madman is the yeoman who has allowed his son to become a gentleman. Lear screams: "To have a thousand with red burning spirits. Come hissing in upon 'em,"--while Edgar shrieks that the foul fiend bites his back. At this the fool remarks that one can not believe "in the tameness of a wolf, a horse's health, a boy's love, or a whore's oath." Then Lear imagines he is judging his daughters. "Sit thou here, most learned justicer," says he, addressing the naked Edgar; "Thou, sapient sir, sit here. Now, you she foxes." To this Edgar says: "Look where he stands and glares! Wantest thou eyes at trial, madam?" "Come o'er the bourn, Bessy, to me,----" while the fool sings:

"Her boat hath a leak And she must not speak Why she dares not come over to thee."

Edgar goes on in his own strain. Kent suggests that Lear should lie down, but Lear continues his imaginary trial: "Bring in their evidence," he cries. "Thou robed man of justice, take thy place," he says to Edgar, "and thou" (to the fool) "his yoke-fellow of equity, bench by his side. You are o' the commission, sit you too," addressing Kent.

"Purr, the cat is gray," shouts Edgar.

"Arraign her first, 'tis Goneril," cries Lear. "I here take my oath before this honorable assembly, she kicked the poor king, her father."

"Come hither, mistress. Is your name Goneril?" says the fool, addressing the seat.

"And here's another," cries Lear. "Stop her there! arms, arms, sword, fire! Corruption in the place! False justice, why hast thou let her 'scape?"

This raving terminates by Lear falling asleep and Gloucester persuading Kent, still without recognizing him, to carry Lear to Dover, and Kent and the fool carry off the King.

The scene is transferred to Gloucester's castle. Gloucester himself is about to be accused of treason. He is brought forward and bound. The Duke of Cornwall plucks out one of his eyes and sets his foot on it. Regan says, "One side will mock another; the other too." The Duke wishes to pluck the other out also, but some servant, for some reason, suddenly takes Gloucester's part and wounds the Duke. Regan kills the servant, who, dying, says to Gloucester that he has "one eye left to see some mischief on him." The Duke says, "Lest it see more, prevent it," and he tears out Gloucester's other eye and throws it on the ground. Here Regan says that it was Edmund who betrayed his father and then Gloucester immediately understands that he has been deceived and that Edgar did not wish to kill him.

Thus ends the third act.

The fourth act is again on the heath. Edgar, still attired as a lunatic, soliloquizes in stilted terms about the instability of fortune and the advantages of a humble lot. Then there comes to him somehow into the very place on the heath where he is, his father, the blinded Gloucester, led by an old man. In that characteristic Shakespearean language,--the chief peculiarity of which is that the thoughts are bred either by the consonance or the contrasts of words,--Gloucester also speaks about the instability of fortune. He tells the old man who leads him to leave him, but the old man points out to him that he can not *see* his way. Gloucester says he has no way and therefore does not require *eyes*. And he argues about his having stumbled when he *saw*, and about defects often proving commodities. "Ah! dear son Edgar," he adds, "might I but live to *see* thee in my touch, I'd say I had *eyes* again." Edgar naked, and in the character of a lunatic, hearing this, still does not disclose himself to his father. He takes the place of the aged guide and talks with his father, who does not recognize his voice, but regards him as a wandering madman. Gloucester avails himself of the opportunity to deliver himself of a witticism: "'Tis the times' plague when madmen lead the blind," and he insists on dismissing the old man, obviously not from motives which might be natural to Gloucester at that moment, but merely in order, when left alone with Edgar, to enact the later scene of the imaginary leaping from the cliff.

Notwithstanding Edgar has just seen his blinded father, and has learnt that his father repents of having banished him, he puts in utterly unnecessary interjections which Shakespeare might know, having read them in Haronet's book, but which Edgar had no means of becoming acquainted with, and above all, which it was quite unnatural for him to repeat in his present position. He says, "Five friends have been in poor Tom at once: of lust, as Obidient; Hobbididance, prince of dumbness; Mahu, of stealing; Modo, of murder; Flibbertigibbet, of mopping and mowing; who since possesses chambermaids and waiting women."

Hearing these words, Gloucester makes a present of his purse to Edgar, saying:

"That I am so wretched Makes thee the happier; heavens, deal so still, Let the superfluous and lust-dieted man, That slaves your ordinance, that will not see Because he doth not feel, feel your power quickly. So distribution should undo excess, And each man have enough."

Having pronounced these strange words, the blind Gloucester requests Edgar to lead him to a certain cliff overhanging the sea, and they depart.

The second scene of the fourth act takes place before the Duke of Albany's palace. Goneril is not only cruel, but also depraved. She despises her husband and discloses her love to the villain Edmund, who has inherited the title of his father Gloucester. Edmund leaves, and a conversation takes place between Goneril and her husband. The Duke of Albany, the only figure with human feelings, who had already previously been dissatisfied with his wife's treatment of her father, now resolutely takes Lear's side, but expresses his emotion in such words as to shake one's confidence in his feeling. He says that a bear would lick Lear's reverence, that if the heavens do not send their visible spirits to tame these vile offenses, humanity must prey on itself like monsters, etc.

Goneril does not listen to him, and then he begins to abuse her:

"See thyself, devil! Proper deformity seems not in the fiend So horrid as in woman."

"O vain fool," says Goneril. "Thou changed and self-cover'd thing, for shame," continues the Duke:

"Be-monster not thy feature. Were't my fitness To let these hands obey my blood, They are apt enough to dislocate and tear Thy flesh and bones; howe'er thou art a fiend, A woman's shape doth shield thee."

After this a messenger enters, and announces that the Duke of Cornwall, wounded by his servant whilst plucking out Gloucester's eyes, had died. Goneril is glad but already anticipates with fear that

Regan, now a widow, will deprive her of Edmund. Here the second scene ends.

The third scene of the fourth act represents the French camp. From a conversation between Kent and a gentleman, the reader or spectator learns that the King of France is not in the camp and that Cordelia has received a letter from Kent and is greatly grieved by what she has learned about her father. The gentleman says that her face reminded one of sunshine and rain.

"Her smiles and tears Were like a better day; those happy smiles That play'd on her ripe lip seem'd not to know What guests were in her eyes; which parted thence, As pearls from diamonds dropp'd."

And so forth.

The gentleman says that Cordelia desires to see her father, but Kent says that Lear is ashamed of seeing this daughter whom he has treated so unkindly.

In the fourth scene, Cordelia, talking with a physician, tells him that Lear has been seen, that he is quite mad, wearing on his head a wreath of various weeds, that he is roaming about and that she has sent soldiers in search of him, adding that she desires all secret remedies to spring with her tears, and the like.

She is informed that the forces of the Dukes are approaching, but she is concerned only about her father and departs.

The fifth scene of the fourth act lies in Gloucester's castle. Regan is talking with Oswald, Goneril's steward, who is carrying a letter from Goneril to Edmund, and she announces to him that she also loves Edmund and that, being a widow, it is better for her to marry him than for Goneril to do so, and she begs him to persuade her sister of this. Further she tells him that it was very unreasonable to blind Gloucester and yet leave him alive, and therefore advises Oswald, should he meet Gloucester, to kill him, promising him a great reward if he does this.

In the sixth scene, Gloucester again appears with his still unrecognized son Edgar, who (now in the guise of a peasant) pretends to lead his father to the cliff. Gloucester is walking along on level land but Edgar persuades him that they are with difficulty ascending a steep hill. Gloucester believes this. Edgar tells his father that the noise of the sea is heard; Gloucester believes this also. Edgar stops on a level place and persuades his father that he has ascended the cliff and that in front of him lies a dreadful abyss, and leaves him alone. Gloucester, addressing the gods, says that he shakes off his affliction as he can bear it no longer, and that he does not condemn them--the gods. Having said this, he leaps on the level ground and falls, imagining that he has jumped off the cliff. On this occasion, Edgar, soliloquizing, gives vent to a yet more entangled utterance:

"I know not how conceit may rob The treasury of life when life itself Yields to the theft; had he been where he thought, By this had thought been past."

He approaches Gloucester, in the character of yet a different person, and expressing astonishment at the latter not being hurt by his fall from such a dreadful height. Gloucester believes that he has fallen and prepares to die, but he feels that he is alive and begins to doubt that he has fallen from such a height. Then Edgar persuades him that he has indeed jumped from the dreadful height and tells him that the individual who had been with him at the top was the devil, as he had eyes like two full moons and a thousand noses and wavy horns. Gloucester believes this, and is persuaded that his despair was the work of the devil, and therefore decides that he will henceforth despair no more, but will quietly await death. Hereupon enters Lear, for some reason covered with wild-flowers. He has lost his senses and says things wilder than before. He speaks about coining, about the moon, gives some one a yard--then he cries that he sees a mouse, which he wishes to entice by a piece of cheese. Then he suddenly demands the password from Edgar, and Edgar immediately answers him with the words "Sweet marjoram." Lear says, "Pass," and the blind Gloucester, who has not recognized either his son or Kent, recognizes the King's voice.

Then the King, after his disconnected utterances, suddenly begins to speak ironically about flatterers, who agreed to all he said, "Ay, and no, too, was no good divinity," but, when he got into a storm without shelter, he saw all this was not true; and then goes on to say that as all creation addicts itself to adultery, and Gloucester's bastard son had treated his father more kindly than his daughters had treated him (altho Lear, according to the development of the drama, could not know how Edmund had treated Gloucester), therefore, let dissoluteness prosper, the more so as, being a King, he needs soldiers. He here addresses an imaginary hypocritically virtuous lady who acts the prude, whereas

"The fitchew nor the soiled horse goes to't With a more riotous appetite. All women inherit the gods only to the girdle Beneath is all the fiend's"--

and, saying this, Lear screams and spits from horror. This monolog is evidently meant to be addressed by the actor to the audience, and probably produces an effect on the stage, but it is utterly uncalled for in the mouth of Lear, equally with his words: "It smells of mortality," uttered while wiping his hand, as Gloucester expresses a desire to kiss it. Then Gloucester's blindness is referred to, which gives occasion for a play of words on *eyes*, about blind Cupid, at which Lear says to Gloucester, "No *eyes* in your head, nor no money in your *purse*? Your *eyes* are in a *heavy* case, your purse in a *light*." Then Lear declaims a monolog on the unfairness of legal judgment, which is quite out of place in the mouth of the insane Lear. After this, enter a gentleman with attendants sent by Cordelia to fetch her father. Lear continues to act as a madman and runs away. The gentleman sent to fetch Lear, does not run after him, but lengthily describes to Edgar the position of the French and British armies. Oswald enters, and seeing Gloucester, and desiring to receive the reward promised by Regan, attacks him, but Edgar with his club kills Oswald, who, in dying, transmits to his murderer, Edgar, Goneril's letter to Edmund, the delivery of which would insure reward. In this letter Goneril promises to kill her husband and marry

Edmund. Edgar drags out Oswald's body by the legs and then returns and leads his father away.

The seventh scene of the fourth act takes place in a tent in the French camp. Lear is asleep on a bed. Enter Cordelia and Kent, still in disguise. Lear is awakened by the music, and, seeing Cordelia, does not believe she is a living being, thinks she is an apparition, does not believe that he himself is alive. Cordelia assures him that she is his daughter, and begs him to bless her. He falls on his knees before her, begs her pardon, acknowledges that he is as old and foolish, says he is ready to take poison, which he thinks she has probably prepared for him, as he is persuaded she must hate him. ("For your sisters," he says, "have done me wrong: you have some cause, they have not.") Then he gradually comes to his senses and ceases to rave. His daughter suggests that he should take a walk. He consents and says: "You must bear with me. Pray you now forget and forgive: I am old and foolish." They depart. The gentleman and Kent, remaining on the scene, hold a conversation which explains to the spectator that Edmund is at the head of the troops and that a battle must soon begin between Lear's defenders and his enemies. So the fourth act closes.

In this fourth act, the scene between Lear and his daughter might have been touching if it had not been preceded in the course of the earlier acts by the tediously drawn out, monotonous ravings of Lear, and if, moreover, this expression of his feelings constituted the last scene. But the scene is not the last.

In the fifth act, the former coldly pompous, artificial ravings of Lear go on again, destroying the impression which the previous scene might have produced.

The first scene of the fifth act at first represents Edmund and Regan; the latter is jealous of her sister and makes an offer. Then come Goneril, her husband, and some soldiers. The Duke of Albany, altho pitying Lear, regards it as his duty to fight with the French who have invaded his country, and so he prepares for battle.

Then Edgar enters, still disguised, and hands to the Duke of Albany the letter he had received from Goneril's dying steward, and tells him if he gains the victory to sound the trumpet, saying that he can produce a champion who will confirm the contents of the letter.

In the second scene, Edgar enters leading his father Gloucester, seats him by a tree, and goes away himself. The noise of battle is heard, Edgar runs back and says that the battle is lost and Lear and Cordelia are prisoners. Gloucester again falls into despair. Edgar, still without disclosing himself to his father, counsels endurance, and Gloucester immediately agrees with him.

The third scene opens with a triumphal progress of the victor Edmund. Lear and Cordelia are prisoners. Lear, altho no longer insane, continues to utter the same senseless, inappropriate words, as, for example, that in prison he will sing with Cordelia, she will ask his blessing, and he will kneel down (this process of kneeling down is repeated three times) and will ask her forgiveness. And he further says that, while they are living in prison, they will wear out "packs and sects of great ones"; that he and Cordelia are sacrifices upon which the gods will throw incense, and that he that parts them "shall bring a brand from heaven and fire them like foxes; that he will not weep, and that the plague shall sooner devour his eyes, flesh and fell, than they shall make them weep."

Edmund orders Lear and his daughter to be led away to prison, and, having called the officer to do this, says he requires another duty and asks him whether he'll do it? The captain says he can not draw a cart nor eat dried oats, but if it be men's work he can do it. Enter the Duke of Albany, Goneril, and Regan. The Duke of Albany wishes to champion Lear, but Edmund does not allow it. The daughters take part in the dialog and begin to abuse each other, being jealous of Edmund. Here everything becomes so confused that it is difficult to follow the action. The Duke of Albany wishes to arrest Edmund, and tells Regan that Edmund has long ago entered into guilty relations with his wife, and that, therefore, Regan must give up her claims on Edmund, and if she wishes to marry, should marry him, the Duke of Albany.

Having said this, the Duke of Albany calls Edmund, orders the trumpet to be sounded, saying that, if no one appears, he will fight him himself.

Here Regan, whom Goneril has evidently poisoned, falls deadly sick. Trumpets are sounded and Edgar enters with a vizor concealing his face, and, without giving his name, challenges Edmund. Edgar abuses Edmund; Edmund throws all the abuses back on Edgar's head. They fight and Edmund falls. Goneril is in despair. The Duke of Albany shows Goneril her letter. Goneril departs.

The dying Edmund discovers that his opponent was his brother. Edgar raises his vizor and pronounces a moral lesson to the effect that, having begotten his illegitimate son Edmund, the father has paid for it with his eyesight. After this Edgar tells the Duke of Albany his adventures and how he has only just now, before entering on the recent combat, disclosed everything to his father, and the father could not bear it and died from emotion. Edmund is not yet dead, and wants to know all that has taken place.

Then Edgar relates that, while he was sitting over his father's body, a man came and closely embraced him, and, shouting as loudly as if he wished to burst heaven, threw himself on the body of Edgar's father, and told the most piteous tale about Lear and himself, and that while relating this the strings of life began to crack, but at this moment the trumpet sounded twice and Edgar left him "tranced"--and this was Kent.

Edgar has hardly finished this narrative when a gentleman rushes in with a bloody knife, shouting "Help!" In answer to the question, "Who is killed?" the gentleman says that Goneril has been killed, having poisoned her sister, she has confessed it.

Enters Kent, and at this moment the corpses of Goneril and Regan are brought in. Edmund here says that the sisters evidently loved him, as one has poisoned the other for his sake, and then slain herself. At the same time he confesses that he had given orders to kill Lear and to hang Cordelia in prison, and pretend that she had taken her own life; but now he wishes to prevent these deeds, and having said this he dies, and is carried away.

After this enters Lear with the dead Cordelia in his arms, altho he is more than eighty years old and ill. Again begins Lear's awful ravings, at which one feels ashamed as at unsuccessful jokes. Lear demands that all should howl, and, alternately, believes that Cordelia is dead and that she is alive.

"Had I your tongues and eyes," he says "I'd use them so that heaven's vault should crack."

Then he says that he killed the slave who hanged Cordelia. Next he says that his eyes see badly, but at the same time he recognizes Kent whom all along he had not recognized.

The Duke of Albany says that he will resign during the life of Lear and that he will reward Edgar and Kent and all who have been faithful to him. At this moment the news is brought that Edmund is dead, and Lear, continuing his ravings, begs that they will undo one of his buttons--the same request which he had made when roaming about the heath. He expresses his thanks for this, tells everyone to look at something, and thereupon dies.

In conclusion, the Duke of Albany, having survived the others, says:

"The weight of this sad time we must obey; Speak what we feel, not what we ought to say. The oldest hath borne most: we that are young Shall never see so much, nor live so long."

All depart to the music of a dead march. Thus ends the fifth act and the drama.

III

Such is this celebrated drama. However absurd it may appear in my rendering (which I have endeavored to make as impartial as possible), I may confidently say that in the original it is yet more absurd. For any man of our time--if he were not under the hypnotic suggestion that this drama is the height of perfection--it would be enough to read it to its end (were he to have sufficient patience for this) to be convinced that far from being the height of perfection, it is a very bad, carelessly composed production, which, if it could have been of interest to a certain public at a certain time, can not evoke among us anything but aversion and weariness. Every reader of our time, who is free from the influence of suggestion, will also receive exactly the same impression from all the other extolled dramas of Shakespeare, not to mention the senseless, dramatized tales, "Pericles," "Twelfth Night," "The Tempest," "Cymbeline," "Troilus and Cressida."

But such free-minded individuals, not inoculated with Shakespeare-worship, are no longer to be found in our Christian society. Every man of our society and time, from the first period of his conscious life, has been inoculated with the idea that Shakespeare is a genius, a poet, and a dramatist, and that all his writings are the height of perfection. Yet, however hopeless it may seem, I will endeavor to demonstrate in the selected drama--"King Lear"--all those faults equally characteristic also of all the other tragedies and comedies of Shakespeare, on account of which he not only is not representing a model of dramatic art, but does not satisfy the most elementary demands of art recognized by all.

Dramatic art, according to the laws established by those very critics who extol Shakespeare, demands that the persons represented in the play should be, in consequence of actions proper to their characters, and owing to a natural course of events, placed in positions requiring them to struggle with the surrounding world to which they find themselves in opposition, and in this struggle should display their inherent qualities.

In "King Lear" the persons represented are indeed placed externally in opposition to the outward world, and they struggle with it. But their strife does not flow from the natural course of events nor from their own characters, but is quite arbitrarily established by the author, and therefore can not produce on the reader the illusion which represents the essential condition of art.

Lear has no necessity or motive for his abdication; also, having lived all his life with his daughters, has no reason to believe the words of the two elders and not the truthful statement of the youngest; yet upon this is built the whole tragedy of his position.

Similarly unnatural is the subordinate action: the relation of Gloucester to his sons. The positions of Gloucester and Edgar flow from the circumstance that Gloucester, just like Lear, immediately believes the coarsest untruth and does not even endeavor to inquire of his injured son whether what he is accused of be true, but at once curses and banishes him. The fact that Lear's relations with his daughters are the same as those of Gloucester to his sons makes one feel yet more strongly that in both cases the relations are quite arbitrary, and do not flow from the characters nor the natural course of events. Equally unnatural, and obviously invented, is the fact that all through the tragedy Lear does not recognize his old courtier, Kent, and therefore the relations between Lear and Kent fail to excite the sympathy of the reader or spectator. The same, in a yet greater degree, holds true of the position of Edgar, who, unrecognized by any one, leads his blind father and persuades him that he has leapt off a cliff, when in reality Gloucester jumps on level ground.

These positions, into which the characters are placed quite arbitrarily, are so unnatural that the reader or spectator is unable not only to sympathize with their sufferings but even to be interested in what he reads or sees. This in the first place.

Secondly, in this, as in the other dramas of Shakespeare, all the characters live, think, speak, and act quite unconformably with the given time and place. The action of "King Lear" takes place 800 years B.C., and yet the characters are placed in conditions possible only in the Middle Ages: participating in the drama are kings, dukes, armies, and illegitimate children, and gentlemen, courtiers, doctors, farmers, officers, soldiers, and knights with vizors, etc. It is possible that such anachronisms (with which Shakespeare's dramas abound) did not injure the possibility of illusion in the sixteenth century and the beginning of the seventeenth, but in our time it is no longer possible to follow with interest the development of events which one knows could not take place in the conditions which the author describes in detail. The artificiality of the positions, not flowing from the natural course of events, or from the nature of the characters, and their want of conformity with time and space, is further increased by those coarse embellishments which are continually added by Shakespeare and intended to appear particularly touching. The extraordinary storm during which King Lear roams about the heath, or the grass which for some reason he puts on his head--like Ophelia in "Hamlet"--or Edgar's attire, or the fool's speeches, or the appearance of the helmeted horseman, Edgar--all these effects not only fail to enhance the impression, but produce an opposite effect. "Man sieht die Absicht und man wird verstimmt," as Goethe says. It often happens that even during these obviously intentional efforts after effect, as, for instance, the dragging out by the legs of half a dozen corpses, with which all Shakespeare's tragedies terminate, instead of feeling fear and pity, one is tempted rather to laugh.

IV

But it is not enough that Shakespeare's characters are placed in tragic positions which are impossible, do not flow from the course of events, are inappropriate to time and space--these personages, besides this, act in a way which is out of keeping with their definite character, and is quite arbitrary. It is generally asserted that in Shakespeare's dramas the characters are specially well expressed, that, notwithstanding their vividness, they are many-sided, like those of living people; that, while exhibiting the characteristics of a given individual, they at the same time wear the features of man in general; it is usual to say that the delineation of character in Shakespeare is the height of perfection.

This is asserted with such confidence and repeated by all as indisputable truth; but however much I endeavored to find confirmation of this in Shakespeare's dramas, I always found the opposite. In reading any of Shakespeare's dramas whatever, I was, from the very first, instantly convinced that he was lacking in the most important, if not the only, means of portraying characters: individuality of language, *i.e.*, the style of speech of every person being natural to his character. This is absent from Shakespeare. All his characters speak, not their own, but always one and the same Shakespearian, pretentious, and unnatural language, in which not only they could not speak, but in which no living man ever has spoken or does speak.

No living men could or can say, as Lear says, that he would divorce his wife in the grave should Regan not receive him, or that the heavens would crack with shouting, or that the winds would burst, or that the wind wishes to blow the land into the sea, or that the curled waters wish to flood the shore, as the gentleman describes the storm, or that it is easier to bear one's grief and the soul leaps over many sufferings when grief finds fellowship, or that Lear has become childless while I am fatherless, as Edgar says, or use similar unnatural expressions with which the speeches of all the characters in all Shakespeare's dramas overflow.

Again, it is not enough that all the characters speak in a way in which no living men ever did or could speak--they all suffer from a common intemperance of language. Those who are in love, who are preparing for death, who are fighting, who are dying, all alike speak much and unexpectedly about subjects utterly inappropriate to the occasion, being evidently guided rather by consonances and play of words than by thoughts. They speak all alike. Lear raves exactly as does Edgar when feigning madness. Both Kent and the fool speak alike. The words of one of the personages might be placed in the mouth of another, and by the character of the speech it would be impossible to distinguish who speaks. If there is a difference in the speech of Shakespeare's various characters, it lies merely in the different dialogs which are pronounced for these characters--again by Shakespeare and not by themselves. Thus Shakespeare always speaks for kings in one and the same inflated, empty language. Also in one and the same Shakespearian, artificially sentimental language speak all the women who are intended to be poetic: Juliet, Desdemona, Cordelia, Imogen, Marina. In the same way, also, it is Shakespeare alone who speaks for his villains: Richard, Edmund, Iago, Macbeth, expressing for them those vicious feelings which villains never express. Yet more similar are the speeches of the madmen with their horrible words, and those of fools with their mirthless puns. So that in Shakespeare there is no language of living individuals--that language which in the drama is the chief means of setting forth character. If gesticulation be also a means of expressing character, as in ballets, this is only a secondary means. Moreover, if the characters speak at random and in a random way, and all in one and the same diction, as is the case in Shakespeare's work, then even the action of gesticulation is wasted. Therefore, whatever the blind panegyrists of Shakespeare may say, in Shakespeare there is no expression of character. Those personages who, in his dramas, stand out as characters, are characters borrowed by him from former works which have served as the foundation of his dramas, and they are mostly depicted, not by the dramatic method which consists in making each person speak with his own diction, but in the epic method of one person describing the features of another.

The perfection with which Shakespeare expresses character is asserted chiefly on the ground of the characters of Lear, Cordelia, Othello, Desdemona, Falstaff, and Hamlet. But all these characters, as well as all the others, instead of belonging to Shakespeare, are taken by him from dramas, chronicles, and romances anterior to him. All these characters not only are not rendered more powerful by him, but, in most cases, they are weakened and spoilt. This is very striking in this drama of "King Lear," which we are examining, taken by him from the drama "King Leir," by an unknown author. The characters of this drama, that of King Lear, and especially of Cordelia, not only were not created by Shakespeare, but have been strikingly weakened and deprived of force by him, as compared with their appearance in the older drama.

In the older drama, Leir abdicates because, having become a widower, he thinks only of saving his soul. He asks his daughters as to their love for him--that, by means of a certain device he has invented, he may retain his favorite daughter on his island. The elder daughters are betrothed, while the youngest does not wish to contract a loveless union with any of the neighboring suitors whom Leir proposes to her, and he is afraid that she may marry some distant potentate.

The device which he has invented, as he informs his courtier, Perillus (Shakespeare's Kent), is this, that when Cordelia tells him that she loves him more than any one or as much as her elder sisters do, he will tell her that she must, in proof of her love, marry the prince he will indicate on his island. All these motives for Lear's conduct are absent in Shakespeare's play. Then, when, according to the old drama, Leir asks his daughters about their love for him, Cordelia does not say, as Shakespeare has it, that she will not give her father all her love, but will love her husband, too, should she marry--which is quite unnatural--but simply says that she can not express her love in words, but hopes that her actions will prove it. Goneril and Regan remark that Cordelia's answer is not an answer, and that the father can not meekly accept such indifference, so that what is wanting in Shakespeare--*i.e.*, the explanation of Lear's anger which caused him to disinherit his youngest daughter,--exists in the old drama. Leir is annoyed by the failure of his scheme, and the poisonous words of his eldest daughters irritate him still more. After the division of the kingdom between the elder daughters, there follows in the older drama a scene between Cordelia and the King of Gaul, setting forth, instead of the colorless Cordelia of Shakespeare, a very definite and attractive character of the truthful, tender, and self-sacrificing youngest daughter. While Cordelia, without grieving that she has been deprived of a portion of the heritage, sits sorrowing at having lost her father's love, and looking forward to earn her bread by her labor, there comes the King of Gaul, who, in the disguise of a pilgrim, desires to choose a bride from among Leir's daughters. He asks Cordelia why she is sad. She tells him the cause of her grief. The King of Gaul, still in the guise of a pilgrim, falls in love with her, and offers to arrange a marriage for her with the King of Gaul, but she says she will marry only a man whom she loves. Then the pilgrim, still disguised, offers her his hand and heart and Cordelia confesses she loves the pilgrim and consents to marry him, notwithstanding the poverty that awaits her. Then the pilgrim discloses to her that he it is who is the King of Gaul, and Cordelia marries him. Instead of this scene, Lear, according to Shakespeare, offers Cordelia's two suitors to take her without dowry, and one cynically refuses, while the other, one does not know why, accepts her. After this, in the old drama, as in Shakespeare's, Leir undergoes the insults of Goneril, into whose house he has removed, but he bears these insults in a very different way from that represented by Shakespeare: he feels that by his conduct toward Cordelia, he has deserved this, and humbly submits. As in Shakespeare's drama, so also in the older drama, the courtiers, Perillus--Kent--who had interceded for Cordelia and was therefore banished--comes to Leir and assures him of his love, but under no disguise, but simply as a faithful old servant who does not abandon his king in a moment of need. Leir tells him what, according to Shakespeare, he tells Cordelia in the last scene, that, if the daughters whom he has benefited hate him, a retainer to whom he has done no good can not love him. But Perillus--Kent--assures the King of his love toward him, and Leir, pacified, goes on to Regan. In the older drama there are no tempests nor tearing out of gray hairs, but there is the weakened and humbled old man, Leir, overpowered with grief, and banished by his other daughter also, who even wishes to kill him. Turned out by his elder daughters, Leir, according to the older drama, as a last resource, goes with Perillus to Cordelia. Instead of the unnatural banishment of Lear during the tempest, and his roaming about the heath, Leir, with Perillus, in the older drama, during their journey to France, very naturally reach the last degree of destitution, sell their clothes in order to pay for their crossing over the sea, and, in the attire of fishermen, exhausted by cold and hunger, approach Cordelia's house. Here, again, instead of the unnatural combined ravings of the fool, Lear, and Edgar, as represented by Shakespeare, there follows in the older drama a natural scene of reunion between the daughter and the father. Cordelia--who, notwithstanding her happiness, has all the time been grieving about her father and praying to God to forgive her sisters who had done him so much wrong--meets her father in his extreme want, and wishes immediately to disclose herself to him, but her husband advises her not to do this, in order not to agitate her weak father. She accepts the counsel and takes Leir into her house without disclosing herself to him, and nurses him. Leir gradually revives, and then the daughter asks him who he is and how he lived formerly:

"If from the first," says Leir, "I should relate the cause, I would make a heart of adamant to weep. And thou, poor soul, kind-hearted as thou art, Dost weep already, ere I do begin."

Cordelia: "For God's love tell it, and when you have done I'll tell the reason why I weep so soon."

And Leir relates all he has suffered from his elder daughters, and says that now he wishes to find shelter with the child who would be in the right even were she to condemn him to death. "If, however," he says, "she will receive me with love, it will be God's and her work, but not my merit." To this Cordelia says: "Oh, I know for certain that thy daughter will lovingly receive thee."--"How canst thou know this without knowing her?" says Leir. "I know," says Cordelia, "because not far from here, I had a father who acted toward me as badly as thou hast acted toward her, yet, if I were only to see his white head, I would creep to meet him on my knees."--"No, this can not be," says Leir, "for there are no children in the world so cruel as mine."--"Do not condemn all for the sins of some," says Cordelia, and falls on her knees. "Look here, dear father," she says, "look on me: I am thy loving daughter." The father recognizes her and says: "It is not for thee, but for me, to beg thy pardon on my knees for all my sins toward thee."

Is there anything approaching this exquisite scene in Shakespeare's drama?

However strange this opinion may seem to worshipers of Shakespeare, yet the whole of this old drama is incomparably and in every respect superior to Shakespeare's adaptation. It is so, first, because it has not got the utterly superfluous characters of the villain Edmund and unlifelike Gloucester and Edgar, who only distract one's attention; secondly because it has not got the completely false "effects" of Lear running about the heath, his conversations with the fool, and all these impossible disguises, failures to recognize, and accumulated deaths; and, above all, because in this drama there is the simple, natural, and deeply touching character of Leir and the yet more touching and clearly defined character of Cordelia, both absent in Shakespeare. Therefore, there is in the older drama, instead of Shakespeare's long-drawn scene of Lear's interview with Cordelia and of Cordelia's unnecessary murder, the exquisite scene of the interview between Leir and Cordelia, unequaled by any in all Shakespeare's dramas.

The old drama also terminates more naturally and more in accordance with the moral demands of the spectator than does Shakespeare's, namely, by the King of the Gauls conquering the husbands of the elder sisters, and Cordelia, instead of being killed, restoring Leir to his former position.

Thus it is in the drama we are examining, which Shakespeare has borrowed from the drama "King Leir." So it is also with Othello, taken from an Italian romance, the same also with the famous Hamlet. The same with Antony, Brutus, Cleopatra, Shylock, Richard, and all Shakespeare's characters, all taken from some antecedent work. Shakespeare, while profiting by characters already given in preceding dramas, or romances, chronicles, or, Plutarch's "Lives," not only fails to render them more truthful and vivid, as his eulogists affirm, but, on the contrary, always weakens them and often completely destroys them, as with Lear, compelling his characters to commit actions unnatural to them, and, above all, to utter speeches natural neither to them nor to any one whatever. Thus, in "Othello," altho that is, perhaps, I will not say the best, but the least bad and the least encumbered by pompous volubility, the characters of Othello, Iago, Cassio, Emilia, according to Shakespeare, are much less natural and lifelike than in the Italian romance. Shakespeare's Othello suffers from epilepsy, of which he has an attack on the stage; moreover, in Shakespeare's version, Desdemona's murder is preceded by the strange vow of the kneeling Othello. Othello, according to Shakespeare, is a negro and not a Moor. All this is erratic, inflated, unnatural, and violates the unity of the character. All this is absent in the romance. In that romance the reasons for Othello's jealousy are represented more naturally than in Shakespeare. In the romance, Cassio, knowing whose the handkerchief is, goes to Desdemona to return it, but, approaching the back-door of Desdemona's house, sees Othello and flies from him. Othello perceives the escaping Cassio, and this, more than anything, confirms his suspicions. Shakespeare has not got this, and yet this casual incident explains Othello's jealousy more than anything else. With Shakespeare, this jealousy is founded entirely on Iago's persistent, successful machinations and treacherous words, which Othello blindly believes. Othello's monolog over the sleeping Desdemona, about his desiring her when killed to look as she is alive, about his going to love her even dead, and now wishing to smell her "balmy breath," etc., is utterly impossible. A man who is preparing for the murder of a beloved being, does not utter such phrases, still less after committing the murder would he speak about the necessity of an eclipse of sun and moon, and of the globe yawning; nor can he, negro tho he may be, address devils, inviting them to burn him in hot sulphur and so forth. Lastly, however effective may be the suicide, absent in the romance, it completely destroys the conception of his clearly defined character. If he indeed suffered from grief and remorse, he would not, intending to kill himself, pronounce phrases about his own services, about the pearl, and about his eyes dropping tears "*as fast as the Arabian trees their medicinal gum*"; and yet less about the Turk's beating an Italian and how he, Othello, smote him--*thus!* So that notwithstanding the powerful expression of emotion in Othello when, under the influence of Iago's hints, jealousy rises in him, and again in his scenes with Desdemona, one's conception of Othello's character is constantly infringed by his false pathos and the unnatural speeches he pronounces.

So it is with the chief character, Othello, but notwithstanding its alteration and the disadvantageous features which it is made thereby to present in comparison with the character from which it was taken in the romance, this character still remains a character, but all the other personages are completely spoiled by Shakespeare.

Iago, according to Shakespeare, is an unmitigated villain, deceiver, and thief, a robber who robs Roderigo and always succeeds even in his most impossible designs, and therefore is a person quite apart from real life. In Shakespeare, the motive of his villainy is, first, that Othello did not give him the post he desired; secondly, that he suspects Othello of an intrigue with his wife and, thirdly, that, as he says, he feels a strange kind of love for Desdemona. There are many motives, but they are all vague. Whereas in the romance there is but one simple and clear motive, Iago's passionate love for Desdemona, transmitted into hatred toward her and Othello after she had preferred the Moor to him and resolutely repulsed him. Yet more unnatural is the utterly unnecessary Roderigo whom Iago deceives and robs, promising him Desdemona's love, and whom he forces to fulfil all he commands: to intoxicate Cassio, provoke and then kill Cassio. Emilia, who says anything it may occur to the author to put into her mouth, has not even the slightest semblance of a live character.

"But Falstaff, the wonderful Falstaff," Shakespeare's eulogists will say, "of him, at all events, one can not say that he is not a living character, or that, having been taken from the comedy of an unknown author, it has been weakened."

Falstaff, like all Shakespeare's characters, was taken from a drama or comedy by an unknown author, written on a really living person, Sir John Oldcastle, who had been the friend of some duke. This Oldcastle had once been convicted of heresy, but had been saved by his friend the duke. But afterward he was condemned and burned at the stake for his religious beliefs, which did not conform with Catholicism. It was on this same Oldcastle that an anonymous author, in order to please the Catholic public, wrote a comedy or drama, ridiculing this martyr for his faith and representing him as a good-for-nothing man, the boon companion of the duke, and it is from this comedy that Shakespeare borrowed, not only the character of Falstaff, but also his own ironical attitude toward it. In Shakespeare's first works, when this character appeared, it was frankly called "Oldcastle," but later, in Elizabeth's time, when Protestantism again triumphed, it was awkward to bring out with mockery a martyr in the strife with Catholicism, and, besides, Oldcastle's relatives had protested, and Shakespeare accordingly altered the name of Oldcastle to that of Falstaff, also a historical figure, known for having fled from the field of battle at Agincourt.

Falstaff is, indeed, quite a natural and typical character; but then it is perhaps the only natural and typical character depicted by Shakespeare. And this character is natural and typical because, of all Shakespeare's characters, it alone speaks a language proper to itself. And it speaks thus because it speaks in that same Shakespearian language, full of mirthless jokes and unamusing puns which, being unnatural to all Shakespeare's other characters, is quite in harmony with the boastful, distorted, and depraved character of the drunken Falstaff. For this reason alone does this figure truly represent a definite character. Unfortunately, the artistic effect of this character is spoilt by the fact that it is so repulsive by its gluttony, drunkenness, debauchery, rascality, deceit, and cowardice, that it is difficult to share the feeling of gay humor with which the author treats it. Thus it is with Falstaff.

But in none of Shakespeare's figures is his, I will not say incapacity to give, but utter indifference to giving, his personages a typical character so strikingly manifest as in Hamlet; and in connection with none of Shakespeare's works do we see so strikingly displayed that blind worship of Shakespeare, that unreasoning state of hypnotism owing to which the mere thought even is not admitted that any of Shakespeare's productions can be wanting in genius, or that any of the principal personages in his dramas can fail to be the expression of a new and deeply conceived character.

Shakespeare takes an old story, not bad in its way, relating:

"Avec quelle ruse Amlette qui depuis fut Roy de Dannemarch, vengea la mort de son père Horwendille, occis par Fengon son frère, et autre occurrence de son histoire," or a drama which was written on this theme fifteen years before him. On this subject he writes his own drama, introducing quite inappropriately (as indeed he always does) into the mouth of the principal person all those thoughts of his own which appeared to him worthy of attention. And putting into the mouth of his hero these thoughts: about life (the grave-digger), about death (To be or not to be)--the same which are expressed in his sixty-sixth sonnet--about the theater, about women. He is utterly unconcerned as to the circumstances under which these words are said, and it naturally turns out that the person expressing all these thoughts is a mere phonograph of Shakespeare, without character, whose actions and words do not agree.

In the old legend, Hamlet's personality is quite comprehensible: he is indignant at his mother's and his uncle's deeds, and wishes to revenge himself upon them, but is afraid his uncle may kill him as he had killed his father. Therefore he simulates insanity, desiring to bide his time and observe all that goes on in the palace. Meanwhile, his uncle and mother, being afraid of him, wish to test whether he is feigning or is really mad, and send to him a girl whom he loves. He persists, then sees his mother in private, kills a courtier who was eavesdropping, and convicts his mother of her sin. Afterward he is sent to England, but intercepts letters and, returning from England, takes revenge of his enemies, burning them all.

All this is comprehensible and flows from Hamlet's character and position. But Shakespeare, putting into Hamlet's mouth speeches which he himself wishes to express, and making him commit actions which are necessary to the author in order to produce scenic effects, destroys all that constitutes the character of Hamlet and of the legend. During the whole of the drama, Hamlet is doing, not what he would really wish to do, but what is necessary for the author's plan. One moment he is awe-struck at his father's ghost, another moment he begins to chaff it, calling it "old mole"; one moment he loves Ophelia, another moment he teases her, and so forth. There is no possibility of finding any explanation whatever of Hamlet's actions or words, and therefore no possibility of attributing any character to him.

But as it is recognized that Shakespeare the genius can not write anything bad, therefore learned people use all the powers of their minds to find extraordinary beauties in what is an obvious and crying failure, demonstrated with especial vividness in "Hamlet," where the principal figure has no character whatever. And lo! profound critics declare that in this drama, in the person of Hamlet, is expressed singularly powerful, perfectly novel, and deep personality, existing in this person having no character; and that precisely in this absence of character consists the genius of creating a deeply conceived character. Having decided this, learned critics write volumes upon volumes, so that the praise and explanation of the greatness and importance of the representation of the character of a man who has no character form in volume a library. It is true that some of the critics timidly express the idea that there is something strange in this figure, that Hamlet is an unsolved riddle, but no one has the courage to say (as in Hans Andersen's story) that the King is naked--*i.e.*, that it is as clear as day that Shakespeare did not succeed and did not even wish to give any character to Hamlet, did not even understand that this was necessary. And learned critics continue to investigate and extol this puzzling production, which reminds one of the famous stone with an inscription which Pickwick found near a cottage doorstep, and which divided the scientific world into two hostile camps.

So that neither do the characters of Lear nor Othello nor Falstaff nor yet Hamlet in any way confirm the existing opinion that Shakespeare's power consists in the delineation of character.

If in Shakespeare's dramas one does meet figures having certain characteristic features, for the most part secondary figures, such as Polonius in "Hamlet" and Portia in "The Merchant of Venice," these few lifelike characters among five hundred or more other secondary figures, with the complete absence of character in the principal figures, do not at all prove that the merit of Shakespeare's dramas consists in the expression of character.

That a great talent for depicting character is attributed to Shakespeare arises from his actually possessing a peculiarity which, for superficial observers and in the play of good actors, may appear to be the capacity of depicting character. This peculiarity consists in the capacity of representative scenes expressing the play of emotion. However unnatural the positions may be in which he places his characters, however improper to them the language which he makes them speak, however featureless they are, the very play of emotion, its increase, and alteration, and the combination of many contrary feelings, as expressed correctly and powerfully in some of Shakespeare's scenes, and in the play of good actors, evokes even, if only for a time, sympathy with the persons represented. Shakespeare, himself an actor, and an intelligent man, knew how to express by the means not only of speech, but of exclamation, gesture, and the repetition of words, states of mind and developments or changes of feeling taking place in the persons represented. So that, in many instances, Shakespeare's characters, instead of speaking, merely make an exclamation, or weep, or in the middle of a monolog, by means of gestures, demonstrate the pain of their position (just as Lear asks some one to unbutton him), or, in moments of great agitation, repeat a question several times, or several times demand the repetition of a word which has particularly struck them, as do Othello, Macduff, Cleopatra, and others. Such clever methods of expressing the development of feeling, giving good actors the possibility of demonstrating their powers, were, and are, often mistaken by many critics for the expression of character. But however strongly the play of feeling may be expressed in one scene, a single scene can not give the character of a figure when this figure, after a correct exclamation or gesture, begins in a language not its own, at the author's arbitrary will, to volubly utter words which are neither necessary nor in harmony with its character.

V

"Well, but the profound utterances and sayings expressed by Shakespeare's characters," Shakespeare's panegyrists will retort. "See Lear's monolog on punishment, Kent's speech about vengeance, or Edgar's about his former life, Gloucester's reflections on the instability of fortune, and, in other dramas, the famous monologs of Hamlet, Antony, and others."

Thoughts and sayings may be appreciated, I will answer, in a prose work, in an essay, a collection of aphorisms, but not in an artistic dramatic production, the object of which is to elicit sympathy with that which is represented. Therefore the monologs and sayings of Shakespeare, even did they contain very many deep and new thoughts, which they do not, do not constitute the merits of an artistic, poetic production. On the contrary, these speeches, expressed in unnatural conditions, can only spoil artistic works.

An artistic, poetic work, particularly a drama, must first of all excite in the reader or spectator the illusion that whatever the person represented is living through, or experiencing, is lived through or experienced by himself. For this purpose it is as important for the dramatist to know precisely what he should make his characters both do and say as what he should not make them say and do, so as not to destroy the illusion of the reader or spectator. Speeches, however eloquent and profound they may be, when put into the mouth of dramatic characters, if they be superfluous or unnatural to the position and character, destroy the chief condition of dramatic art-- the illusion, owing to which the reader or spectator lives in the feelings of the persons represented. Without putting an end to the illusion, one may leave much unsaid--the reader or spectator will himself fill this up, and sometimes, owing to this, his illusion is even increased, but to say what is superfluous is the same as to overthrow a statue composed of separate pieces and thereby scatter them, or to take away the lamp from a magic lantern: the attention of the reader or spectator is distracted, the reader sees the author, the spectator sees the actor, the illusion disappears, and to restore it is sometimes impossible; therefore without the feeling of measure there can not be an artist, and especially a dramatist.

Shakespeare is devoid of this feeling. His characters continually do and say what is not only unnatural to them, but utterly unnecessary. I do not cite examples of this, because I believe that he who does not himself see this striking deficiency in all Shakespeare's dramas will not be persuaded by any examples and proofs. It is sufficient to read "King Lear," alone, with its insanity, murders, plucking out of eyes, Gloucester's jump, its poisonings, and wranglings--not to mention "Pericles," "Cymbeline," "The Winter's Tale," "The Tempest"--to be convinced of this. Only a man devoid of the sense of measure and of taste could produce such types as "Titus Andronicus" or "Troilus and Cressida," or so mercilessly mutilate the old drama "King Leir."

Gervinus endeavors to prove that Shakespeare possessed the feeling of beauty, "Schönheit's sinn," but all Gervinus's proofs prove only that he himself, Gervinus, is completely destitute of it. In Shakespeare everything is exaggerated: the actions are exaggerated, so are their consequences, the speeches of the characters are exaggerated, and therefore at every step the possibility of artistic impression is interfered with. Whatever people may say, however they may be enraptured by Shakespeare's works, whatever merits they may attribute to them, it is perfectly certain that he was not an artist and that his works are not artistic productions. Without the sense of measure, there never was nor can be an artist, as without the feeling of rhythm there can not be a musician. Shakespeare might have been whatever you like, but he was not an artist.

"But one should not forget the time at which Shakespeare wrote," say his admirers. "It was a time of cruel and coarse habits, a time of the then fashionable euphemism, *i.e.*, artificial way of expressing oneself--a time of forms of life strange to us, and therefore, to judge about Shakespeare, one should have in view the time when he wrote. In Homer, as in Shakespeare, there is much which is strange to us, but this does not prevent us from appreciating the beauties of Homer," say these admirers. But in comparing Shakespeare with Homer, as does Gervinus, that infinite distance which separates true poetry from its semblance manifests itself with especial force. However distant Homer is from us, we can, without the slightest effort, transport ourselves into the life he describes, and we can thus transport ourselves because, however alien to us may be the events Homer describes, he believes in what he says and speaks seriously, and therefore he never exaggerates, and the sense of measure never abandons him. This is the reason why, not to speak of the wonderfully distinct, lifelike, and beautiful characters of Achilles, Hector, Priam, Odysseus, and the eternally touching scenes of Hector's leave-taking, of Priam's embassy, of Odysseus's return, and others--the whole of the "Iliad" and still more the "Odyssey" are so humanly near to us that we feel as if we ourselves had lived, and are living, among its gods and heroes. Not so with Shakespeare. From his first words, exaggeration is seen: the exaggeration of events, the exaggeration of emotion, and the exaggeration of effects. One sees at once that he does not believe in what he says, that it is of no necessity to him, that he invents the events he describes, and is indifferent to his characters--that he has conceived them only for the stage and therefore makes them do and say only what may strike his public; and therefore we do not believe either in the events, or in the actions, or in the sufferings of the characters. Nothing demonstrates so clearly the complete absence of esthetic feeling in Shakespeare as comparison between him and Homer. The works which we call the works of Homer are artistic, poetic, original works, lived through by the author or authors; whereas the works of Shakespeare--borrowed as they are, and, externally, like mosaics, artificially fitted together piecemeal from bits invented for the occasion--have nothing whatever in common with art and poetry.

But, perhaps, the height of Shakespeare's conception of life is such that, tho he does not satisfy the esthetic demands, he discloses to us a view of life so new and important for men that, in consideration of its importance, all his failures as an artist become imperceptible. So, indeed, say Shakespeare's admirers. Gervinus says distinctly that besides Shakespeare's significance in the sphere of dramatic poetry in which, according to his opinion, Shakespeare equals "Homer in the sphere of Epos, Shakespeare being the very greatest judge of the human soul, represents a teacher of most indisputable ethical authority and the most select leader in the world and in life."

In what, then, consists this indisputable authority of the most select leader in the world and in life? Gervinus devotes the concluding chapter of his second volume, about fifty pages, to an explanation of this.

The ethical authority of this supreme teacher of life consists in the following: The starting point of Shakespeare's conception of life, says Gervinus, is that man is gifted with powers of activity, and therefore, first of all, according to Gervinus, Shakespeare regarded it as good and necessary for man that he should act (as if it were possible for a man not to act):

"Die thatkräftigen Männer, Fortinbras, Bolingbroke, Alcibiades, Octavius spielen hier die gegensätzlichen Rollen gegen die verschiedenen thatlosen; nicht ihre Charaktere verdienen ihnen Allen ihr Glück und Gedeihen etwa durch eine grosse Ueberlegenheit ihrer Natur, sondern trotz ihrer geringeren Anlage stellt sich ihre Thatkraft an sich über die Unthätigkeit der Anderen hinaus, gleichviel aus wie schöner Quelle diese Passivität, aus wie schlechter jene Thätigkeit fliesse."

I.e., active people, like Fortinbras, Bolingbroke, Alcibiades, Octavius, says Gervinus, are placed in contrast, by Shakespeare, with various characters who do not exhibit energetic activity. And happiness and success, according to Shakespeare, are attained by individuals possessing this active character, not at all owing to the superiority of their nature; on the contrary, notwithstanding their inferior gifts, the capacity of activity itself always gives them the advantage over inactivity, quite independent of any consideration whether the inactivity of some persons flows from excellent impulses and the activity of others from bad ones. "Activity is good, inactivity is evil. Activity transforms evil into good," says Shakespeare, according to Gervinus. Shakespeare prefers the principle of Alexander (of Macedonia) to that of Diogenes, says Gervinus. In other words, he prefers death and murder due to ambition, to abstinence and wisdom.

According to Gervinus, Shakespeare believes that humanity need not set up ideals, but that only healthy activity and the golden mean are necessary in everything. Indeed, Shakespeare is so penetrated by this conviction that, according to Gervinus's assertion, he allows himself to deny even Christian morality, which makes exaggerated demands on human nature. Shakespeare, as we read, did not approve of limits of duty exceeding the intentions of nature. He teaches the golden mean between heathen hatred to one's enemies and Christian love toward them (pp. 561, 562). How far Shakespeare was penetrated with this fundamental principle of *reasonable moderation*, says Gervinus, can be seen from the fact that he has the courage to express himself even against the Christian rules which prompt human nature to the excessive exertion of its powers. He did not admit that the limits of duties should exceed the biddings of Nature. Therefore he preached a reasonable mean natural to man, between Christian and heathen precepts, of love toward one's enemies on the one hand, and hatred toward them on the other.

That one may do too much good (exceed the reasonable limits of good) is convincingly proved by Shakespeare's words and examples. Thus excessive generosity ruins Timon, while Antonio's moderate generosity confers honor; normal ambition makes Henry V. great, whereas it ruins Percy, in whom it has risen too high; excessive virtue leads Angelo to destruction, and if, in those who surround him, excessive severity becomes harmful and can not prevent crime, on the other hand the divine element in man, even charity, if it be excessive, can create crime.

Shakespeare taught, says Gervinus, that one *may be too good*.

He teaches that morality, like politics, is a matter in which, owing to the complexity of circumstances and motives, one can not establish any principles (p. 563), and in this he agrees with Bacon and Aristotle--there are no positive religious and moral laws which may create principles for correct moral conduct suitable for all cases.

Gervinus most clearly expresses the whole of Shakespeare's moral theory by saying that Shakespeare does not write for those classes for whom definite religious principles and laws are suitable (*i.e.*, for nine hundred and ninety-nine one-thousandths of men) but for the educated:

"There are classes of men whose morality is best guarded by the positive precepts of religion and state law; to such persons Shakespeare's creations are inaccessible. They are comprehensible and accessible only to the educated, from whom one can expect that they should acquire the healthy tact of life and self-consciousness by means of which the innate guiding powers of conscience and reason, uniting with the will, lead us to the definite attainment of worthy aims in life. But even for such educated people, Shakespeare's teaching is not always without danger. The condition on which his teaching is quite harmless is that it should be accepted in all its completeness, in all its parts, without any omission. Then it is not only without danger, but is the most clear and faultless and therefore the most worthy of confidence of all moral teaching" (p. 564).

In order thus to accept all, one should understand that, according to his teaching, it is stupid and harmful for the individual to revolt against, or endeavor to overthrow, the limits of established religious and state forms. "Shakespeare," says Gervinus, "would abhor an independent and free individual who, with a powerful spirit, should struggle against all convention in politics and morality and overstep that union between religion and the State which has for thousands of years supported society. According to his views, the practical wisdom of men could not have a higher object than the introduction into society of the greatest spontaneity and freedom, but precisely because of this one should safeguard as sacred and irrefragable the natural laws of society--one should respect the existing order of things and, continually verifying it, inculcate its rational sides, not overlooking nature for the sake of culture, or *vice versa*" (p. 566). Property, the family, the state, are sacred; but aspiration toward the recognition of the equality of men is insanity. Its realization would bring humanity to the greatest calamities. No one struggled more than Shakespeare against the privileges of rank and position, but could this freethinking man resign himself to the privileges of the wealthy and educated being destroyed in order to give room to the poor and ignorant? How could a man who so eloquently attracts people toward honors, permit that the very aspiration toward that which was great be crushed together with rank and distinction for services, and, with the destruction of all degrees, "the motives for all high undertakings be stifled"? Even if the attraction of honors and false power treacherously obtained were to cease, could the poet admit of the most dreadful of all violence, that of the ignorant crowd? He saw that, thanks to this equality now preached, everything may pass into violence, and violence into arbitrary acts and thence into unchecked passion which will rend the world as the wolf does its prey, and in the end the world will swallow itself up. Even if this does not happen with mankind when it attains equality--if the love of nations and eternal peace prove not to be that impossible "nothing," as Alonso expressed it in "The Tempest"--but if, on the contrary, the actual attainment of aspirations toward equality is possible, then the poet would deem that the old age and extinction of the world had approached, and that, therefore, for active individuals, it is not worth while to live (pp. 571, 572).

Such is Shakespeare's view of life as demonstrated by his greatest exponent and admirer.

Another of the most modern admirers of Shakespeare, George Brandes, further sets forth:[2]

"No one, of course, can conserve his life quite pure from evil, from deceit, and from the injury of others, but evil and deceit are not always vices, and even the evil caused to others, is not necessarily a vice: it is often merely a necessity, a legitimate weapon, a right. And indeed, Shakespeare always held that there are no unconditional prohibitions, nor unconditional duties. For instance, he did not doubt Hamlet's right to kill the King, nor even his right to stab Polonius to death, and yet he could not restrain himself from an overwhelming feeling of indignation and repulsion when, looking around, he saw everywhere how incessantly the most elementary moral laws were being infringed. Now, in his mind there was formed, as it were, a closely riveted ring of thoughts concerning which he had always vaguely felt: such unconditional commandments do not exist; the quality and significance of an act, not to speak of a character, do not depend upon their enactment or infringement; the whole substance lies in the contents with which the separate individual, at the moment of his decision and on his own responsibility, fills up the form of these laws."

In other words, Shakespeare at last clearly saw that the moral of the *aim* is the only true and possible one; so that, according to Brandes, Shakespeare's fundamental principle, for which he extols him, is that *the end justifies the means*--action at all costs, the absence of all ideals, moderation in everything, the conservation of the forms of life once established, and the end justifying the means. If you add to this a Chauvinist English patriotism, expressed in all the historical dramas, a patriotism according to which the English throne is something sacred, Englishmen always vanquishing the French, killing thousands and losing only scores, Joan of Arc regarded as a witch, and the belief that Hector and all the Trojans, from whom the English came, are heroes, while the Greeks are cowards and traitors, and so forth,--such is the view of life of the wisest teacher of life according to his greatest admirers. And he who will attentively read Shakespeare's works can not fail to recognize that the description of this Shakespearian view of life by his admirers is quite correct.

The merit of every poetic work depends on three things:

(1) The subject of the work: the deeper the subject, *i.e.*, the more important it is to the life of mankind, the higher is the work.

(2) The external beauty achieved by technical methods proper to the particular kind of art. Thus, in dramatic art, the technical method will be a true individuality of language, corresponding to the characters, a natural, and at the same time touching plot, a correct scenic rendering of the demonstration and development of emotion, and the feeling of measure in all that is represented.

(3) Sincerity, *i.e.*, that the author should himself keenly feel what he expresses. Without this condition there can be no work of art, as the essence of art consists in the contemplation of the work of art being infected with the author's feeling. If the author does not actually feel what he expresses, then the recipient can not become infected with the feeling of the author, does not experience any feeling, and the production can no longer be classified as a work of art.

The subject of Shakespeare's pieces, as is seen from the demonstrations of his greatest admirers, is the lowest, most vulgar view of life, which regards the external elevation of the lords of the world as a genuine distinction, despises the crowd, *i.e.*, the working classes--repudiates not only all religious, but also all humanitarian, strivings directed to the betterment of the existing order.

The second condition also, with the exception of the rendering of the scenes in which the movement of feelings is expressed, is quite absent in Shakespeare. He does not grasp the natural character of the positions of his personages, nor the language of the persons represented, nor the feeling of measure without which no work can be artistic.

The third and most important condition, sincerity, is completely absent in all Shakespeare's works. In all of them one sees intentional artifice; one sees that he is not *in earnest*, but that he is playing with words.

VII

Shakespeare's works do not satisfy the demands of all art, and, besides this, their tendency is of the lowest and most immoral. What then signifies the great fame these works have enjoyed for more than a hundred years?

Many times during my life I have had occasion to argue about Shakespeare with his admirers, not only with people little sensitive to poetry, but with those who keenly felt poetic beauty, such as Turgenef, Fet,[3] and others, and every time I encountered one and the same attitude toward my objection to the praises of Shakespeare. I was not refuted when I pointed out Shakespeare's defects; they only condoled with me for my want of comprehension, and urged upon me the necessity of recognizing the extraordinary supernatural grandeur of Shakespeare, and they did not explain to me in what the beauties of Shakespeare consisted, but were merely vaguely and exaggeratedly enraptured with the whole of Shakespeare, extolling some favorite passages: the unbuttoning of Lear's button, Falstaff's lying, Lady Macbeth's ineffaceable spots, Hamlet's exhortation to his father's ghost, "forty thousand brothers," etc.

"Open Shakespeare," I used to say to these admirers, "wherever you like, or wherever it may chance, you will see that you will never find ten consecutive lines which are comprehensible, unartificial, natural to the character that says them, and which produce an artistic impression." (This experiment may be made by any one. And either at random, or according to their own choice.) Shakespeare's admirers opened pages in Shakespeare's dramas, and without paying any attention to my criticisms as to why the selected ten lines did not satisfy the most elementary demands of esthetic and common sense, they were enchanted with the very thing which to me appeared absurd, incomprehensible, and inartistic. So that, in general, when I endeavored to get from Shakespeare's worshipers an explanation of his greatness, I met in them exactly the same attitude which I have met, and which is usually met, in the defenders of any dogmas accepted not through reason, but through faith. It is this attitude of

Shakespeare's admirers toward their object--an attitude which may be seen also in all the mistily indefinite essays and conversations about Shakespeare--which gave me the key to the understanding of the cause of Shakespeare's fame. There is but one explanation of this wonderful fame: it is one of those epidemic "suggestions" to which men constantly have been and are subject. Such "suggestion" always has existed and does exist in the most varied spheres of life. As glaring instances, considerable in scope and in deceitful influence, one may cite the medieval Crusades which afflicted, not only adults, but even children, and the individual "suggestions," startling in their senselessness, such as faith in witches, in the utility of torture for the discovery of the truth, the search for the elixir of life, the philosopher's stone, or the passion for tulips valued at several thousand guldens a bulb which took hold of Holland. Such irrational "suggestions" always have been existing, and still exist, in all spheres of human life--religious, philosophical, political, economical, scientific, artistic, and, in general, literary--and people clearly see the insanity of these suggestions only when they free themselves from them. But, as long as they are under their influence, the suggestions appear to them so certain, so true, that to argue about them is regarded as neither necessary nor possible. With the development of the printing press, these epidemics became especially striking.

With the development of the press, it has now come to pass that so soon as any event, owing to casual circumstances, receives an especially prominent significance, immediately the organs of the press announce this significance. As soon as the press has brought forward the significance of the event, the public devotes more and more attention to it. The attention of the public prompts the press to examine the event with greater attention and in greater detail. The interest of the public further increases, and the organs of the press, competing with one another, satisfy the public demand. The public is still more interested; the press attributes yet more significance to the event. So that the importance of the event, continually growing, like a lump of snow, receives an appreciation utterly inappropriate to its real significance, and this appreciation, often exaggerated to insanity, is retained so long as the conception of life of the leaders of the press and of the public remains the same. There are innumerable examples of such an inappropriate estimation which, in our time, owing to the mutual influence of press and public on one another, is attached to the most insignificant subjects. A striking example of such mutual influence of the public and the press was the excitement in the case of Dreyfus, which lately caught hold of the whole world.

The suspicion arose that some captain of the French staff was guilty of treason. Whether because this particular captain was a Jew, or because of some special internal party disagreements in French society, the press attached a somewhat prominent interest to this event, whose like is continually occurring without attracting any one's attention, and without being able to interest even the French military, still less the whole world. The public turned its attention to this incident, the organs of the press, mutually competing, began to describe, examine, discuss the event; the public was yet more interested; the press answered to the demand of the public, and the lump of snow began to grow and grow, till before our eyes it attained such a bulk that there was not a family where controversies did not rage about "l'affaire." The caricature by Caran d'Ache representing at first a peaceful family resolved to talk no more about Dreyfus, and then, like exasperated furies, members of the same family fighting with each other, quite correctly expressed the attitude of the whole of the reading world to the question about Dreyfus. People of foreign nationalities, who could not be interested in the question whether a French officer was a traitor or not--people, moreover, who could know nothing of the development of the case-- all divided themselves for and against Dreyfus, and the moment they met they talked and argued about Dreyfus, some asserting his guilt with assurance, others denying it with equal assurance. Only after the lapse of some years did people begin to awake from the "suggestion" and to understand that they could not possibly know whether Dreyfus was guilty or not, and that each one had thousands of subjects much more near to him and interesting than the case of Dreyfus.

Such infatuations take place in all spheres, but they are especially noticeable in the sphere of literature, as the press naturally occupies itself the more keenly with the affairs of the press, and they are particularly powerful in our time when the press has received such an unnatural development. It continually happens that people suddenly begin to extol some most insignificant works, in exaggerated language, and then, if these works do not correspond to the prevailing view of life, they suddenly become utterly indifferent to them, and forget both the works themselves and their former attitude toward them.

So within my recollection, in the forties, there was in the sphere of art the laudation and glorification of Eugène Sue, and Georges Sand; and in the social sphere Fourier; in the philosophical sphere, Comte and Hegel; in the scientific sphere, Darwin.

Sue is quite forgotten, Georges Sand is being forgotten and replaced by the writings of Zola and the Decadents, Beaudelaire, Verlaine, Maeterlinck, and others. Fourier with his phalansteries is quite forgotten, his place being taken by Marx. Hegel, who justified the existing order, and Comte, who denied the necessity of religious activity in mankind, and Darwin with his law of struggle, still hold on, but are beginning to be forgotten, being replaced by the teaching of Nietzsche, which, altho utterly extravagant, unconsidered, misty, and vicious in its bearing, yet corresponds better with existing tendencies. Thus sometimes artistic, philosophic, and, in general, literary crazes suddenly arise and are as quickly forgotten. But it also happens that such crazes, having arisen in consequence of special reasons accidentally favoring to their establishment, correspond in such a degree to the views of life spread in society, and especially in literary circles, that they are maintained for a long time. As far back as in the time of Rome, it was remarked that often books have their own very strange fates: consisting in failure notwithstanding their high merits, and in enormous undeserved success notwithstanding their triviality. The saying arose: "pro captu lectoris habent sua fata libelli"--*i.e.*, that the fate of books depends on the understanding of those who read them. There was harmony between Shakespeare's writings and the view of life of those amongst whom his fame arose. And this fame has been, and still is, maintained owing to Shakespeare's works continuing to correspond to the life concept of those who support this fame.

Until the end of the eighteenth century Shakespeare not only failed to gain any special fame in England, but was valued less than his contemporary dramatists: Ben Jonson, Fletcher, Beaumont, and others. His fame originated in Germany, and thence was transferred to England. This happened for the following reason:

Art, especially dramatic art, demanding for its realization great preparations, outlays, and labor, was always religious, *i.e.*, its object was to stimulate in men a clearer conception of that relation of man to God which had, at that time, been attained by the leading men of the circles interested in art.

So it was bound to be from its own nature, and so, as a matter of fact, has it always been among all nations--Egyptians, Hindus, Chinese, Greeks--commencing in some remote period of human life. And it has always happened that, with the coarsening of religious forms, art has more and more diverged from its original object (according to which it could be regarded as an important function-- almost an act of worship), and, instead of serving religious objects, it strove for worldly aims, seeking to satisfy the demands of the crowd or of the powerful, *i.e.*, the aims of recreation and amusement. This deviation of art from its true and high vocation took place everywhere, and even in connection with Christianity.

The first manifestations of Christian art were services in churches: in the administration of the sacraments and the ordinary liturgy. When, in course of time, the forms of art as used in worship became insufficient, there appeared the Mysteries, describing those events which were regarded as the most important in the Christian religious view of life. When, in the thirteenth and fourteenth centuries, the center of gravity of Christian teaching was more and more transferred, the worship of Christ as God, and the interpretation and following of His teaching, the form of Mysteries describing external Christian events became insufficient, and new forms were demanded. As the expression of the aspirations which gave rise to these changes, there appeared the Moralities, dramatic representations in which the characters were personifications of Christian virtues and their opposite vices.

But allegories, owing to the very fact of their being works of art of a lower order, could not replace the former religious dramas, and yet no new forms of dramatic art corresponding to the conception now entertained of Christianity, according to which it was regarded as a teaching of life, had yet been found. Hence, dramatic art, having no foundation, came in all Christian countries to swerve farther and farther from its proper use and object, and, instead of serving God, it took to serving the crowd (by crowd, I mean, not simply the masses of common people, but the majority of immoral or unmoral men, indifferent to the higher problems of human life). This deviation was, moreover, encouraged by the circumstance that, at this very time, the Greek thinkers, poets, and dramatists, hitherto unknown in the Christian world, were discovered and brought back into favor. From all this it followed that, not having yet had time to work out their own form of dramatic art corresponding to the new conception entertained of Christianity as being a teaching of life, and, at the same time, recognizing the previous form of Mysteries and Moralities as insufficient, the writers of the fifteenth and sixteenth centuries, in their search for a new form, began to imitate the newly discovered Greek models, attracted by their elegance and novelty.

Since those who could principally avail themselves of dramatic representations were the powerful of this world: kings, princes, courtiers, the least religious people, not only utterly indifferent to the questions of religion, but in most cases completely depraved-- therefore, in satisfying the demands of its audience, the drama of the fifteenth and sixteenth and seventeenth centuries entirely gave up all religious aim. It came to pass that the drama, which formerly had such a lofty and religious significance, and which can, on this condition alone, occupy an important place in human life, became, as in the time of Rome, a spectacle, an amusement, a recreation--*only* with this difference, that in Rome the spectacles existed for the whole people, whereas in the Christian world of the fifteenth, sixteenth, and seventeenth centuries they were principally meant for depraved kings and the higher classes. Such was the case with the Spanish, English, Italian, and French drama.

The dramas of that time, principally composed, in all these countries, according to ancient Greek models, or taken from poems, legends, or biographies, naturally reflected the characteristics of their respective nationalities: in Italy comedies were chiefly elaborated, with humorous positions and persons. In Spain there flourished the worldly drama, with complicated plots and historical heroes. The peculiarities of the English drama were the coarse incidents of murders, executions, and battles taking place on the stage, and popular, humorous interludes. Neither the Italian nor the Spanish nor the English drama had European fame, but they all enjoyed success in their own countries. General fame, owing to the elegance of its language and the talent of its writers, was possessed only by the French drama, distinguished by its strict adherence to the Greek models, and especially to the law of the three Unities.

So it continued till the end of the eighteenth century, at which time this happened: In Germany, which had not produced even passable dramatic writers (there was a weak and little known writer, Hans Sachs), all educated people, together with Frederick the Great, bowed down before the French pseudo-classical drama. Yet at this very time there appeared in Germany a group of educated and talented writers and poets, who, feeling the falsity and coldness of the French drama, endeavored to find a new and freer dramatic form. The members of this group, like all the upper classes of the Christian world at that time, were under the charm and influence of the Greek classics, and, being utterly indifferent to religious questions, they thought that if the Greek drama, describing the calamities and sufferings and strife of its heroes, represented the highest dramatic ideal, then such a description of the sufferings and the struggles of heroes would be a sufficient subject in the Christian world, too, if only the narrow demands of pseudo-classicalism were rejected. These men, not understanding that, for the Greeks, the strife and sufferings of their heroes had a religious significance, imagined that they needed only to reject the inconvenient law of the three Unities, without introducing into the drama any religious element corresponding to their time, in order that the drama should have sufficient scope in the representation of various moments in the lives of historical personages and, in general, of strong human passions. Exactly this kind of drama existed at that time among the kindred English people, and, becoming acquainted with it, the Germans decided that precisely such should be the drama of the new period.

Thereupon, because of the clever development of scenes which constituted Shakespeare's peculiarity, they chose Shakespeare's dramas in preference to all other English dramas, excluding those which were not in the least inferior, but were even superior, to Shakespeare. At the head of the group stood Goethe, who was then the dictator of public opinion in esthetic questions. He it was who, partly owing to a desire to destroy the fascination of the false French art, partly owing to his desire to give a greater scope to his own dramatic writing, but chiefly through the agreement of his view of life with Shakespeare's, declared Shakespeare a great poet. When this error was announced by an authority like Goethe, all those esthetic critics who did not understand art threw themselves on it like crows on carrion and began to discover in Shakespeare beauties which did not exist, and to extol them. These men, German esthetic critics, for the most part utterly devoid of esthetic feeling, without that simple, direct artistic sensibility which, for people with a feeling for art, clearly distinguishes esthetic impressions from all others, but believing the authority which had recognized Shakespeare as a great poet, began to praise the whole of Shakespeare indiscriminately, especially distinguishing such passages as struck them by their effects, or which expressed thoughts corresponding to their views of life, imagining that these effects and these thoughts constitute the essence of what is called art. These men acted as blind men would act who endeavored to find diamonds by touch among a heap of stones they were fingering. As the blind man would for a long time strenuously handle the stones and in the end would come to no other conclusion than that all stones are precious and especially so the smoothest, so also these esthetic critics, without artistic feeling, could not but come to similar results in relation to Shakespeare. To give the greater force to their praise of the whole of Shakespeare, they invented esthetic theories according to which it appeared that no definite religious view of life was necessary for works of art in general, and especially for the drama; that for the purpose of the drama the representation of human passions and characters was quite sufficient; that not only was an internal religious illumination of what was represented unnecessary, but art should be objective, *i.e.*, should represent events quite independently of any judgment of good and evil. As these theories were founded on Shakespeare's own views of life, it naturally turned out that the works of Shakespeare satisfied these theories and therefore were the height of perfection.

It is these people who are chiefly responsible for Shakespeare's fame. It was principally owing to their writings that the interaction took place between writers and public which expressed itself, and is still expressing itself, in an insane worship of Shakespeare which has no rational foundation. These esthetic critics have written profound treatises about Shakespeare. Eleven thousand volumes have been written about him, and a whole science of Shakespearology composed; while the public, on the one hand, took more and more interest, and the learned critics, on the other hand, gave further and further explanations, adding to the confusion.

So that the first cause of Shakespeare's fame was that the Germans wished to oppose to the cold French drama, of which they had grown weary, and which, no doubt, was tedious enough, a livelier and freer one. The second cause was that the young German writers required a model for writing their own dramas. The third and principal cause was the activity of the learned and zealous esthetic German critics without esthetic feeling, who invented the theory of objective art, deliberately rejecting the religious essence of the drama.

"But," I shall be asked, "what do you understand by the word's religious essence of the drama? May not what you are demanding for the drama, religious instruction, or didactics, be called 'tendency,' a thing incompatible with true art?" I reply that by the religious essence of art I understand not the direct inculcation of any religious truths in an artistic guise, and not an allegorical demonstration of these truths, but the exhibition of a definite view of life corresponding to the highest religious understanding of a given time, which, serving as the motive for the composition of the drama, penetrates, to the knowledge of the author, through all of his work. So it has always been with true art, and so it is with every true artist in general and especially the dramatist. Hence--as it was when the drama was a serious thing, and as it should be according to the essence of the matter--that man alone can write a drama who has something to say to men, and something which is of the greatest importance for them: about man's relation to God, to the Universe, to the All, the Eternal, the Infinite. But when, thanks to the German theories about objective art, the idea was established that, for the drama, this was quite unnecessary, then it is obvious how a writer like Shakespeare--who had not got developed in his mind the religious convictions proper to his time, who, in fact, had no convictions at all, but heaped up in his drama all possible events, horrors, fooleries, discussions, and effects--could appear to be a dramatic writer of the greatest genius.

But these are all external reasons. The fundamental inner cause of Shakespeare's fame was and is this: that his dramas were "pro captu lectoris," *i.e.*, they corresponded to the irreligious and immoral frame of mind of the upper classes of his time.

VIII

At the beginning of the last century, when Goethe was dictator of philosophic thought and esthetic laws, a series of casual circumstances made him praise Shakespeare. The esthetic critics caught up this praise and took to writing their lengthy, misty, learned articles, and the great European public began to be enchanted with Shakespeare. The critics, answering to the popular interest, and endeavoring to compete with one another, wrote new and ever new essays about Shakespeare; the readers and spectators on their side were increasingly confirmed in their admiration, and Shakespeare's fame, like a lump of snow, kept growing and growing, until in our time it has attained that insane worship which obviously has no other foundation than "suggestion."

Shakespeare finds no rival, not even approximately, either among the old or the new writers. Here are some of the tributes paid to him.

"Poetic truth is the brightest flower in the crown of Shakespeare's merits;" "Shakespeare is the greatest moralist of all times;" "Shakespeare exhibits such many-sidedness and such objectivism that they carry him beyond the limits of time and nationality;" "Shakespeare is the greatest genius that has hitherto existed;" "For the creation of tragedy, comedy, history, idyll, idyllistic comedy, esthetic idyll, for the profoundest presentation, or for any casually thrown off, passing piece of verse, he is the only man. He not only wields an unlimited power over our mirth and our tears, over all the workings of passion, humor, thought, and observation, but he possesses also an infinite region full of the phantasy of fiction, of a horrifying and an amusing character. He possesses penetration both in the world of fiction and of reality, and above this reigns one and the same truthfulness to character and to nature, and the same spirit of humanity;" "To Shakespeare the epithet of Great comes of itself; and if one adds that independently of his greatness he has, further, become the reformer of all literature, and, moreover, has in his works not only expressed the phenomenon of life as it was in his day, but also, by the genius of thought which floated in the air has prophetically forestalled the direction that the social spirit was going to take in the future (of which we see a striking example in

Hamlet),--one may, without hesitation, say that Shakespeare was not only a great poet, but the greatest of all poets who ever existed, and that in the sphere of poetic creation his only worthy rival was that same life which in his works he expressed to such perfection."

The obvious exaggeration of this estimate proves more conclusively than anything that it is the consequence, not of common sense, but of suggestion. The more trivial, the lower, the emptier a phenomenon is, if only it has become the subject of suggestion, the more supernatural and exaggerated is the significance attributed to it. The Pope is not merely saintly, but most saintly, and so forth. So Shakespeare is not merely a good writer, but the greatest genius, the eternal teacher of man kind.

Suggestion is always a deceit, and every deceit is an evil. In truth, the suggestion that Shakespeare's works are great works of genius, presenting the height of both esthetic and ethical perfection, has caused, and is causing, great injury to men.

This injury is twofold: first, the fall of the drama, and the replacement of this important weapon of progress by an empty and immoral amusement; and secondly, the direct depravation of men by presenting to them false models for imitation.

Human life is perfected only through the development of the religious consciousness, the only element which permanently unites men. The development of the religious consciousness of men is accomplished through all the sides of man's spiritual activity. One direction of this activity is in art. One section of art, perhaps the most influential, is the drama.

Therefore the drama, in order to deserve the importance attributed to it, should serve the development of religious consciousness. Such has the drama always been, and such it was in the Christian world. But upon the appearance of Protestantism in its broader sense, *i.e.*, the appearance of a new understanding of Christianity as of a teaching of life, the dramatic art did not find a form corresponding to the new understanding of Christianity, and the men of the Renaissance were carried away by the imitation of classical art. This was most natural, but the tendency was bound to pass, and art had to discover, as indeed it is now beginning to do, its new form corresponding to the change in the understanding of Christianity.

But the discovery of this new form was arrested by the teaching arising among German writers at the end of the eighteenth and beginning of the nineteenth centuries--as to so-called objective art, *i.e.*, art indifferent to good or evil--and therein the exaggerated praise of Shakespeare's dramas, which partly corresponded to the esthetic teaching of the Germans, and partly served as material for it. If there had not been exaggerated praise of Shakespeare's dramas, presenting them as the most perfect models, the men of the eighteenth and nineteenth centuries would have had to understand that the drama, to have a right to exist and to be a serious thing, must serve, as it always has served and can not but do otherwise, the development of the religious consciousness. And having understood this, they would have searched for a new form of drama corresponding to their religious understanding.

But when it was decided that the height of perfection was Shakespeare's drama, and that we ought to write as he did, not only without any religious, but even without any moral, significance, then all writers of dramas in imitation of him began to compose such empty pieces as are those of Goethe, Schiller, Hugo, and, in Russia, of Pushkin, or the chronicles of Ostrovski, Alexis Tolstoy, and an innumerable number of other more or less celebrated dramatic productions which fill all the theaters, and can be prepared wholesale by any one who happens to have the idea or desire to write a play. It is only thanks to such a low, trivial understanding of the significance of the drama that there appears among us that infinite quantity of dramatic works describing men's actions, positions, characters, and frames of mind, not only void of any spiritual substance, but often of any human sense.

Let not the reader think that I exclude from this estimate of contemporary drama the theatrical pieces I have myself incidentally written. I recognize them, as well as all the rest, as not having that religious character which must form the foundation of the drama of the future.

The drama, then, the most important branch of art, has, in our time, become the trivial and immoral amusement of a trivial and immoral crowd. The worst of it is, moreover, that to dramatic art, fallen as low as it is possible to fall, is still attributed an elevated significance no longer appropriate to it. Dramatists, actors, theatrical managers, and the press--this last publishing in the most serious tone reports of theaters and operas--and the rest, are all perfectly certain that they are doing something very worthy and important.

The drama in our time is a great man fallen, who has reached the last degree of his degradation, and at the same time continues to pride himself on his past of which nothing now remains. The public of our time is like those who mercilessly amuse themselves over this man once so great and now in the lowest stage of his fall.

Such is one of the mischievous effects of the epidemic suggestion about the greatness of Shakespeare. Another deplorable result of this worship is the presentation to men of a false model for imitation. If people wrote of Shakespeare that for his time he was a good writer, that he had a fairly good turn for verse, was an intelligent actor and good stage manager--even were this appreciation incorrect and somewhat exaggerated--if only it were moderately true, people of the rising generation might remain free from Shakespeare's influence. But when every young man entering into life in our time has presented to him, as the model of moral perfection, not the religious and moral teachers of mankind, but first of all Shakespeare, concerning whom it has been decided and is handed down by learned men from generation to generation, as an incontestable truth, that he was the greatest poet, the greatest teacher of life, the young man can not remain free from this pernicious influence. When he is reading or listening to Shakespeare the question for him is no longer whether Shakespeare be good or bad, but only: In what consists that extraordinary beauty, both esthetic and ethical, of which he has been assured by learned men whom he respects, and which he himself neither sees nor feels? And constraining himself, and distorting his esthetic and ethical feeling, he tries to conform to the ruling opinion. He no longer believes in himself, but in what is said by the learned people whom he respects. I have experienced all this. Then reading critical examinations of the dramas and extracts from books with explanatory comments, he begins to imagine that he feels something of the nature of an artistic impression. The longer this continues, the more does his esthetical and ethical feeling become distorted. He ceases to distinguish directly and clearly what is artistic from an artificial imitation of art. But, above all, having assimilated the immoral view of life which penetrates all Shakespeare's writings, he loses the capacity of distinguishing good from evil. And the error of extolling an insignificant, inartistic writer--not only not moral, but directly immoral--executes its destructive work.

This is why I think that the sooner people free themselves from the false glorification of Shakespeare, the better it will be.

First, having freed themselves from this deceit, men will come to understand that the drama which has no religious element at its foundation is not only not an important and good thing, as it is now supposed to be, but the most trivial and despicable of things. Having understood this, they will have to search for, and work out, a new form of modern drama, a drama which will serve as the development and confirmation of the highest stage of religious consciousness in men.

Secondly, having freed themselves from this hypnotic state, men will understand that the trivial and immoral works of Shakespeare and his imitators, aiming merely at the recreation and amusement of the spectators, can not possibly represent the teaching of life, and that, while there is no true religious drama, the teaching of life should be sought for in other sources.

FOOTNOTES:

[1] This essay owes its origin to Leo Tolstoy's desire to contribute a preface to the article he here mentions by Ernest Crosby, which latter follows in this volume.--(*Trans.*)

[2] "Shakespeare and His Writings," by George Brandes.

[3] A Russian poet, remarkable for the delicacy of his works.

PART II
APPENDIX

APPENDIX CONTENTS

I. SHAKESPEARE'S ATTITUDE TOWARD THE WORKING CLASSES, BY ERNEST CROSBY, 127

II. LETTER FROM MR. G. BERNARD SHAW, 166

SHAKESPEARE'S ATTITUDE TOWARD THE WORKING CLASSES

BY ERNEST CROSBY

"Shakespeare was of us," cries Browning, in his "Lost Leader," while lamenting the defection of Wordsworth from the ranks of progress and liberalism--"Milton was for us, Burns, Shelley were with us--they watch from their graves!" There can, indeed, be no question of the fidelity to democracy of Milton, the republican pamphleteer, nor of Burns, the proud plowman, who proclaimed the fact that "a man's a man for a' that," nor of Shelley, the awakened aristocrat, who sang to such as Burns

"Men of England, wherefore plow For the lords who lay ye low?"

But Shakespeare?--Shakespeare?--where is there a line in Shakespeare to entitle him to a place in this brotherhood? Is there anything in his plays that is in the least inconsistent with all that is reactionary?

A glance at Shakespeare's lists of *dramatis personæ* is sufficient to show that he was unable to conceive of any situation rising to the dignity of tragedy in other than royal and ducal circles. It may be said in explanation of this partiality for high rank that he was only following the custom of the dramatists of his time, but this is a poor plea for a man of great genius, whose business it is precisely to lead and not to follow. Nor is the explanation altogether accurate. In his play, the "Pinner of Wakefield," first printed in 1599, Robert Greene makes a hero, and a very stalwart one, of a mere pound-keeper, who proudly refuses knighthood at the hands of the king. There were other and earlier plays in vogue in Shakespeare's day treating of the triumphs of men of the people, one, for instance, which commemorated the rise of Sir Thomas Gresham, the merchant's son, and another, entitled "The History of Richard Whittington, of his Low Birth, his Great Fortune"; but he carefully avoided such material in seeking plots for his dramas. Cardinal Wolsey, the butcher's son, is indeed the hero of "Henry VIII.," but his humble origin is only mentioned incidentally as something to be ashamed of. What greater opportunity for idealizing the common people ever presented itself to a dramatist than to Shakespeare when he undertook to draw the character of Joan of Arc in the second part of "Henry VI."? He knew how to create noble women--that is one of his special glories--but he not only refuses to see anything noble in the peasant girl who led France to victory, but he deliberately insults her memory with the coarsest and most cruel calumnies. Surely the lapse of more than a century and a half might have enabled a man of honor, if not of genius, to do justice to an enemy of the weaker sex, and if Joan had been a member of the French royal family we may be sure that she would have received better treatment.

The question of the aristocratic tendency of the drama was an active one in Shakespeare's time. There was a good deal of democratic feeling in the burghers of London-town, and they resented the courtly prejudices of their playwrights and their habit of holding up plain citizens to ridicule upon the stage, whenever they deigned to present them at all. The Prolog in Beaumont and Fletcher's "Knight of the Burning Pestle" gives sufficient evidence of this. The authors adopted the device of having a Citizen leap upon the stage and interrupt the Speaker of the Prolog by shouting

"Hold your peace, goodman boy!"

Speaker of Prolog: "What do you mean, sir?"

Citizen: "That you have no good meaning; this seven year there hath been plays at this house. I have observed it, you have still girds at citizens."

The Citizen goes on to inform the Speaker of the Prolog that he is a grocer, and to demand that he "present something notably in honor of the commons of the city." For a hero he will have "a grocer, and he shall do admirable things." But this proved to be a joke over too serious a matter, for at the first representation of the play in 1611 it was cried down by the citizens and apprentices, who did not appreciate its satire upon them, and it was not revived for many years thereafter. It will not answer, therefore, to say that the idea of celebrating the middle and lower classes never occurred to Shakespeare, for it was a subject of discussion among his contemporaries.

It is hardly possible to construct a play with no characters but monarchs and their suites, and at the same time preserve the verisimilitudes of life. Shakespeare was obliged to make some use of servants, citizens, and populace. How has he portrayed them? In one play alone has he given up the whole stage to them, and it is said that the "Merry Wives of Windsor" was only written at the request of Queen Elizabeth, who wished to see Sir John Falstaff in love. It is from beginning to end one prolonged "gird at citizens," and we can hardly wonder that they felt a grievance against the dramatic profession. In the other plays of Shakespeare the humbler classes appear for the main part only occasionally and incidentally. His opinion of them is indicated more or less picturesquely by the names which he selects for them. There are, for example, Bottom, the weaver; Flute, the bellows-maker; Snout and Sly, tinkers; Quince, the carpenter; Snug, the joiner; Starveling, the tailor; Smooth, the silkman; Shallow and Silence, country justices; Elbow and Hull, constables; Dogberry and Verges, Fang and Snare, sheriffs' officers; Mouldy, Shadow, Wart, and Bull-calf, recruits; Feebee, at once a recruit and a woman's tailor, Pilch and Patch-Breech, fishermen (though these last two appellations may be mere nicknames); Potpan, Peter Thump, Simple, Gobbo, and Susan Grindstone, servants; Speed, "a clownish servant"; Slender, Pistol, Nym, Sneak, Doll Tear-sheet, Jane Smile, Costard, Oatcake, Seacoal, and various anonymous "clowns" and "fools." Shakespeare rarely gives names of this character to any but the lowly in life, altho perhaps we should cite as exceptions Sir Toby Belch and Sir Andrew Ague-Cheek in "Twelfth Night"; the vicar, Sir Oliver Mar-Text, in "As You Like It"; Moth, the page, in "Love's Labor Lost," and Froth, "a foolish gentleman," in "Measure for Measure," but none of these personages quite deserves to rank as an aristocrat. Such a system of nomenclature as we have exposed is enough of itself to fasten the stigma of absurdity upon the characters subjected to it, and their occupations. Most of the trades are held up for ridicule in "Midsummer Night's Dream"; Holofernes, the schoolmaster, is made ridiculous in "Love's Labor Lost," and we are told of the middle-class Nym, Pistol, and Bardolph that "three such antics do not amount to a man" (Henry V., Act 3, Sc. 2). But it is not necessary to rehearse the various familiar scenes in which these fantastically named individuals raise a laugh at their own expense.

The language employed by nobility and royalty in addressing those of inferior station in Shakespeare's plays may be taken, perhaps, rather as an indication of the manners of the times than as an expression of his own feeling, but even so it must have been a little galling to the poorer of his auditors. "Whoreson dog," "whoreson peasant," "slave," "you cur," "rogue," "rascal," "dunghill," "crack-hemp," and "notorious villain"--these are a few of the epithets with which the plays abound. The Duke of York accosts Thomas Horner, an armorer, as "base dunghill villain and mechanical" (Henry VI., Part 2, Act 2, Sc. 3); Gloster speaks of the warders of the Tower as "dunghill grooms" (Ib., Part 1, Act 1, Sc. 3), and Hamlet of the grave-digger as an "ass" and "rude knave." Valentine tells his servant, Speed, that he is born to be hanged (Two Gentlemen of Verona, Act 1, Sc. 1), and Gonzalo pays a like compliment to the boatswain who is doing his best to save the ship in the "Tempest" (Act 1, Sc. 1). This boatswain is not sufficiently impressed by the grandeur of his noble cargo, and for his pains is called a "brawling, blasphemous, uncharitable dog," a "cur," a "whoreson, insolent noise-maker," and a "wide-chapped rascal." Richard III.'s Queen says to a gardener, who is guilty of nothing but giving a true report of her lord's deposition and who shows himself a kind-hearted fellow, "Thou little better thing than earth," "thou wretch"! Henry VIII. talks of a "lousy footboy," and the Duke of Suffolk, when he is about to be killed by his pirate captor at Dover, calls him "obscure and lowly swain," "jaded groom," and "base slave," dubs his crew "paltry, servile, abject drudges," and declares that his own head would

"sooner dance upon bloody pole Than stand uncovered to a vulgar groom." (Henry VI., Part 2, Act 4, Sc. 1.)

Petruchio "wrings Grumio by the ear," and Katherine beats the same unlucky servant. His master indulges in such terms as "foolish knave," "peasant swain," and "whoreson malthorse drudge" in addressing him; cries out to his servants, "off with my boots, you rogues, you villains!" and strikes them. He pays his compliments to a tailor in the following lines:

"O monstrous arrogance! Thou liest, thou thread, thou thimble, Thou yard, three-quarters, half-yard, quarter, nail, Thou flea, thou nit, thou winter cricket thou; Braved in my own house by a skein of thread! Away, thou rag, thou quantity, thou remnant!" (Taming of the Shrew, Act 4, Sc. 3.)

Joan of Arc speaks of her "contemptible estate" as a shepherd's daughter, and afterward, denying her father, calls him "Decrepit miser! base, ignoble wretch!" (Henry VI., Part 1, Act 1, Sc. 2, and Act 5, Sc. 4.) It is hard to believe that Shakespeare would have so frequently allowed his characters to express their contempt for members of the lower orders of society if he had not had some sympathy with their opinions.

Shakespeare usually employs the common people whom he brings upon the stage merely to raise a laugh (as, for instance, the flea-bitten carriers in the inn-yard at Rochester, in Henry IV., Part 1, Act 2, Sc. 1), but occasionally they are scamps as well as fools. They amuse us when they become hopelessly entangled in their sentences (*vide* Romeo and Juliet, Act 1, Sc. 2), or when Juliet's nurse blunderingly makes her think that Romeo is slain instead of Tybalt; but when this same lady, after taking Romeo's money, espouses the cause of the County Paris--or when on the eve of Agincourt we are introduced to a group of cowardly English soldiers--or when Coriolanus points out the poltroonery of the Roman troops, and says that all would have been lost "but for our gentlemen," we must feel detestation for them. Juliet's nurse is not the only disloyal servant. Shylock's servant, Launcelot Gobbo, helps Jessica to deceive her father, and Margaret, the Lady Hero's gentlewoman, brings about the disgrace of her mistress by fraud. Olivia's waiting-woman in "Twelfth Night" is honest enough, but she is none too modest in her language, but in this respect Dame Quickly in "Henry IV." can easily rival her. Peter Thump, when forced to a judicial combat with his master, displays his cowardice, altho in the end he is successful (Henry VI., Act 2, Part 2, Sc. 3), and Stephano, a drunken butler, adorns the stage in the "Tempest." We can not blame Shakespeare for making use of cutthroats and villains in developing his plots, but we might have been spared the jokes which the jailors of Posthumus perpetrate when they come to lead him to the scaffold, and the ludicrous English of the clown who supplies Cleopatra with an asp. The apothecary who is in such wretched plight that he sells poison to Romeo in spite of a Draconian law, gives us another unflattering picture of a tradesman; and when Falstaff declares, "I would I were a weaver; I could sing psalms or anything," we have a premature reflection on the Puritan, middle-class conscience and religion. In "As You Like It," Shakespeare came near drawing a pastoral sketch of shepherds and shepherdesses on conventional lines. If he failed to do so, it was as much from lack of respect for the keeping of sheep as for the unrealities of pastoral poetry. Rosalind does not scruple to call the fair Phebe "foul," and, as for her hands, she says:

"I saw her hand; she has a leathern hand, A freestone colored hand; I verily did think That her old gloves were on, but 'twas her hands; She has a housewife's hand."

No one with a high respect for housewifery could have written that line. When in the same play Jaques sees the pair of rural lovers, Touchstone and Audrey, approaching, he cries: "There is, sure, another flood, and these couples are coming to the ark! Here come a pair of very strange beasts, which in all tongues are called fools" (Act 5, Sc. 4). The clown, Touchstone, speaks of kissing the cow's dugs which his former sweetheart had milked, and then marries Audrey in a tempest of buffoonery. Howbeit, Touchstone remains one of the few rustic characters of Shakespeare who win our affections, and at the same time he is witty enough to deserve the title which Jaques bestows upon him of a "rare fellow."

Occasionally Shakespeare makes fun of persons who are somewhat above the lower classes in rank. I have mentioned those on whom he bestows comical names. He indulges in humor also at the expense of the two Scottish captains, Jamy and Macmorris, and the honest Welsh captain, Fluellen (Henry V., Act 3, Sc. 2 *et passim*), and shall we forget the inimitable Falstaff? But, while making every allowance for these diversions into somewhat nobler quarters (the former of which are explained by national prejudices), do they form serious exceptions to the rule, and can Falstaff be taken, for instance, as a representative of the real aristocracy? As Queen and courtiers watched his antics on the stage, we may be sure that it never entered their heads that the "girds" were directed at them or their kind.

The appearance on Shakespeare's stage of a man of humble birth who is virtuous without being ridiculous is so rare an event that it is worth while to enumerate the instances. Now and then a servant or other obscure character is made use of as a mere lay figure of which nothing good or evil can be predicated, but usually they are made more or less absurd. Only at long intervals do we see persons of this class at once serious and upright. As might have been expected, it is more often the servant than any other member of the lower classes to whom Shakespeare attributes good qualities, for the servant is a sort of attachment to the gentleman and shines with the reflection of his virtues. The noblest quality which Shakespeare can conceive of in a servant is loyalty, and in "Richard II." (Act 5, Sc. 3) he gives us a good example in the character of a groom who remains faithful to the king even when the latter is cast into prison. In "Cymbeline" we are treated to loyalty *ad nauseam*. The king orders Pisanio, a trusty servant, to be tortured without cause, and his reply is,

"Sir, my life is yours. I humbly set it at your will." (Act 4, Sc. 3.)

In "King Lear" a good servant protests against the cruelty of Regan and Cornwall toward Gloucester, and is killed for his courage. "Give me my sword," cries Regan. "A peasant stand up thus!" (Act 3, Sc. 7). And other servants also show sympathy for the unfortunate earl. We all remember the fool who, almost alone, was true to Lear, but, then, of course, he was a fool. In "Timon of Athens" we have an unusual array of good servants, but it is doubtful if Shakespeare wrote the play, and these characters make his authorship more doubtful. Flaminius, Timon's servant, rejects a bribe with scorn (Act 3, Sc. 1). Another of his servants expresses his contempt for his master's false friends (Act 3, Sc. 3), and when Timon finally loses his fortune and his friends forsake him, his servants stand by him. "Yet do our hearts wear Timon's livery" (Act 4, Sc. 2). Adam, the good old servant in "As You Like It," who follows his young master Orlando into exile, is, like Lear's fool, a noteworthy example of the loyal servitor.

"Master, go on, and I will follow thee To the last gasp with truth and loyalty." (Act 2, Sc. 3.)

But Shakespeare takes care to point out that such fidelity in servants is most uncommon and a relic of the good old times--

"O good old man, bow well in thee appears The constant service of the antique world, When service sweat for duty, nor for meed! Thou art not for the fashion of these times, When none will sweat but for promotion."

Outside the ranks of domestic servants we find a few cases of honorable poverty in Shakespeare. In the play just quoted, Corin, the old shepherd, says:

"Sir, I am a true laborer; I earn that I eat, get that I wear; owe no man hate, envy no man's happiness; glad of other men's good, content with my harm; and the greatest of my pride is to see my ewes graze and my lambs suck." (As You Like It, Act 3, Sc. 2.)

in short, an ideal proletarian from the point of view of the aristocrat.

The "Winter's Tale" can boast of another good shepherd (Act 3, Sc. 3), but he savors a little of burlesque. "Macbeth" has several humble worthies. There is a good old man in the second act (Sc. 2), and a good messenger in the fourth (Sc. 2). King Duncan praises highly the sergeant who brings the news of Macbeth's victory, and uses language to him such as Shakespeare's yeomen are not accustomed to hear (Act 1, Sc. 2). And in "Antony and Cleopatra" we make the acquaintance of several exemplary common soldiers. Shakespeare puts flattering words into the mouth of Henry V. when he addresses the troops before Agincourt:

"For he to-day that sheds his blood with me Shall be my brother; be he ne'er so vile This day shall gentle his condition." (Act 4, Sc. 4.)

And at Harfleur he is even more complaisant:

"And you, good yeomen, Whose limbs were made in England, shew us here The metal of your pasture; let us swear That you are worth your breeding; which I doubt not, For there is none of you so mean and base That hath not noble luster in your eyes." (Act 3, Sc. 1.)

The rank and file always fare well before a battle.

"Oh, it's 'Tommy this' and 'Tommy that' an' 'Tommy, go away'; But it's 'Thank you, Mr. Atkins,' when the band begins to play."

I should like to add some instances from Shakespeare's works of serious and estimable behavior on the part of individuals representing the lower classes, or of considerate treatment of them on the part of their "betters," but I have been unable to find any, and the meager list must end here.

But to return to Tommy Atkins. He is no longer Mr. Atkins after the battle. Montjoy, the French herald, comes to the English king under a flag of truce and asks that they be permitted to bury their dead and

"Sort our nobles from our common men; For many of our princes (wo the while!) Lie drowned and soaked in mercenary blood; So do our vulgar drench their peasant limbs In blood of princes." (Henry V., Act 4, Sc. 7.)

With equal courtesy Richard III., on Bosworth field, speaks of his opponents to the gentlemen around him:

"Remember what you are to cope withal-- A sort of vagabonds, rascals, and runaways, A scum of Bretagne and base lackey peasants." (Act 5, Sc. 3.)

But Shakespeare does not limit such epithets to armies. Having, as we have seen, a poor opinion of the lower classes, taken man by man, he thinks, if anything, still worse of them taken *en masse*, and at his hands a crowd of plain workingmen fares worst of all. "Hempen home-spuns," Puck calls them, and again

"A crew of patches, rude mechanicals, That work for bread upon Athenian stalls."

Bottom, their leader, is, according to Oberon, a "hateful fool," and according to Puck, the "shallowest thick-skin of that barren sort" (Midsummer Night's Dream, Act 3, Scs. 1 and 2, Act 4, Sc. 1). Bottom's advice to his players contains a small galaxy of compliments:

"In any case let Thisby have clean linen, and let not him that plays the lion pare his nails, for they shall hang out for the lion's claws. And, most dear actors, eat no onion or garlic, for we are to utter sweet breath, and I do not doubt to hear them say, it is a sweet comedy." (Ib., Act 4, Sc. 2.)

The matter of the breath of the poor weighs upon Shakespeare and his characters. Cleopatra shudders at the thought that

"mechanic slaves, With greasy aprons, rules and hammers, shall Uplift us to the view; in their thick breaths Rank of gross diet, shall we be enclouded, And forced to drink their vapor." (Antony and Cleopatra, Act 5, Sc. 2.)

Coriolanus has his sense of smell especially developed. He talks of the "stinking breaths" of the people (Act 2, Sc. 1), and in another place says:

"You common cry of curs, whose breath I hate As reek of rotten fens, whose love I prize As the dead carcasses of unburied men That do corrupt the air, I banish you,"

and he goes on to taunt them with cowardice (Act 3, Sc. 3). They are the "mutable, rank-scented many" (Act 3, Sc. 1). His friend Menenius is equally complimentary to his fellow citizens. "You are they," says he,

"That make the air unwholesome, when you cast Your stinking, greasy caps, in hooting at Coriolanus's exile." (Act 4, Sc. 7.)

And he laughs at the "apron-men" of Cominius and their "breath of garlic-eaters" (Act 4, Sc. 7). When Coriolanus is asked to address the people, he replies by saying: "Bid them wash their faces, and keep their teeth clean" (Act 2, Sc. 3). According to Shakespeare, the Roman populace had made no advance in cleanliness in the centuries between Coriolanus and Cæsar. Casca gives a vivid picture of the offer of the crown to Julius, and his rejection of it: "And still as he refused it the rabblement shouted, and clapped their chapped hands, and threw up their sweaty night-caps, and uttered such a deal of stinking breath, because Cæsar refused the crown, that it had almost choked Cæsar, for he swooned and fell down at it. And for mine own part I durst not laugh, for fear of opening my lips and receiving the bad air." And he calls them the "tag-rag people" (Julius Cæsar, Act 1, Sc. 2). The play of "Coriolanus" is a mine of insults to the people and it becomes tiresome to quote them. The hero calls them the "beast with many heads" (Act 4, Sc. 3), and again he says to the crowd:

"What's the matter, you dissentious rogues, That rubbing the poor itch of your opinion Make yourself scabs?

First Citizen. We have ever your good word.

Coriolanus. He that will give good words to ye will flatter Beneath abhorring. What would you have, you curs, That like not peace nor war? The one affrights you, The other makes you proud. He that trusts to you, Where he would find you lions, finds you hares; Where foxes, geese; you are no surer, no, Than is the coal of fire upon the ice, Or hailstone in the sun. Your virtue is To make him worthy whose offense subdues him, And curse that justice did it. Who deserves greatness Deserves your hate; and your affections are A sick man's appetite, who desires most that Which would increase his evil. He that depends Upon your favors, swims with fins of lead, And hews down oaks with rushes. Hang ye! Trust ye? With every minute you do change a mind, And call him noble that was now your hate, Him vile that was your garland." (Act 1, Sc. 1.)

His mother, Volumnia, is of like mind. She calls the people "our general louts" (Act 3, Sc. 2). She says to Junius Brutus, the tribune of the people:

"'Twas you incensed the rabble, Cats, that can judge as fitly of his worth As I can of those mysteries which Heaven Will not leave Earth to know." (Act 4, Sc. 2).

In the same play Cominius talks of the "dull tribunes" and "fusty plebeians" (Act 1, Sc. 9). Menenius calls them "beastly plebeians" (Act 2, Sc. 1), refers to their "multiplying spawn" (Act 2, Sc. 2), and says to the crowd:

"Rome and her rats are at the point of battle." (Act 1, Sc. 2).

The dramatist makes the mob cringe before Coriolanus. When he appears, the stage directions show that the "citizens steal away." (Act 1, Sc. 1.)

As the Roman crowd of the time of Coriolanus is fickle, so is that of Cæsar's. Brutus and Antony sway them for and against his assassins with ease:

"First Citizen. This Cæsar was a tyrant.

Second Citizen. Nay, that's certain. We are blessed that Rome is rid of him....

First Citizen. (After hearing a description of the murder.) O piteous spectacle!

2 Cit. O noble Cæsar!

3 Cit. O woful day!

4 Cit. O traitors, villains!

1 Cit. O most bloody sight!

2 Cit. We will be revenged; revenge! about--seek--burn, fire--kill--slay--let not a traitor live!" (Act 3, Sc. 2.)

The Tribune Marullus reproaches them with having forgotten Pompey, and calls them

"You blocks, you stones, you worse than senseless things."

He persuades them not to favor Cæsar, and when they leave him he asks his fellow tribune, Flavius,

"See, whe'r their basest metal be not moved?" (Act 1, Sc. 1.)

Flavius also treats them with scant courtesy:

"Hence, home, you idle creatures, get you home. Is this a holiday? What! you know not, Being mechanical, you ought not walk Upon a laboring day without the sign Of your profession?" (Ib.)

The populace of England is as changeable as that of Rome, if Shakespeare is to be believed. The Archbishop of York, who had espoused the cause of Richard II. against Henry IV., thus soliloquizes:

"The commonwealth is sick of their own choice; Their over greedy love hath surfeited; An habitation giddy and unsure Hath he that buildeth on the vulgar heart. O thou fond many! With what loud applause Didst thou beat Heaven with blessing Bolingbroke, Before he was what thou would'st have him be! And now being trimmed in thine own desires, Thou, beastly feeder, art so full of him, That thou provokest thyself to cast him up. So, so, thou common dog, didst thou disgorge Thy glutton bosom of the royal Richard, And now thou wouldst eat thy dead vomit up, And howlst to find it." (Henry IV., Part 2, Act 1, Sc. 3.)

Gloucester in "Henry VI." (Part 2, Act 2, Sc. 4) notes the fickleness of the masses. He says, addressing his absent wife:

"Sweet Nell, ill can thy noble mind abrook The abject people, gazing on thy face With envious looks, laughing at thy shame, That erst did follow thy proud chariot wheels When thou didst ride in triumph through the streets."

When she arrives upon the scene in disgrace, she says to him:

"Look how they gaze; See how the giddy multitude do point And nod their heads and throw their eyes on thee. Ah, Gloster, hide thee from their hateful looks."

And she calls the crowd a "rabble" (Ib.), a term also used in "Hamlet" (Act 4, Sc. 5). Again, in part III. of "Henry VI.," Clifford, dying on the battlefield while fighting for King Henry, cries:

"The common people swarm like summer flies, And whither fly the gnats but to the sun? And who shines now but Henry's enemies?" (Act 2, Sc. 6.)

And Henry himself, conversing with the keepers who have imprisoned him in the name of Edward IV., says:

"Ah, simple men! you know not what you swear. Look, as I blow this feather from my face, And as the air blows it to me again, Obeying with my wind when I do blow, And yielding to another when it blows, Commanded always by the greater gust, Such is the lightness of you common men." (Ib., Act 3, Sc. 1.)

Suffolk, in the First Part of the same trilogy (Act 5, Sc. 5), talks of "worthless peasants," meaning, perhaps, "property-less peasants," and when Salisbury comes to present the demands of the people, he calls him

"the Lord Ambassador Sent from a sort of tinkers to the king," (Part 2, Act 3, Sc. 2.)

and says:

"'Tis like the Commons, rude unpolished hinds Could send such message to their sovereign."

Cardinal Beaufort mentions the "uncivil kernes of Ireland" (Ib., Part 2, Act 3, Sc. 1), and in the same play the crowd makes itself ridiculous by shouting, "A miracle," when the fraudulent beggar Simpcox, who had pretended to be lame and blind, jumps over a stool to escape a whipping (Act 2, Sc. 1). Queen Margaret receives petitioners with the words "Away, base cullions" (Ib., Act 1, Sc. 3), and among other flattering remarks applied here and there to the lower classes we may cite the epithets "ye rascals, ye rude slaves," addressed to a crowd by a porter in Henry VIII., and that of "lazy knaves" given by the Lord Chamberlain to the porters for having let in a "trim rabble" (Act 5, Sc. 3). Hubert, in King John, presents us with an unvarnished picture of the common people receiving the news of Prince Arthur's death:

"I saw a smith stand with his hammer, thus, The whilst his iron did on his anvil cool, With open mouth swallowing a tailor's news; Who, with his shears and measure in his hand, Standing on slippers (which his nimble haste Had falsely thrust upon contrary feet), Told of a many thousand warlike French That were embattailed and rank'd in Kent. Another lean, unwashed artificer, Cuts off his tale, and talks of Arthur's death." (Act 4, Sc. 2.)

Macbeth, while sounding the murderers whom he intends to employ, and who say to him, "We are men, my liege," answers:

"Ay, in the catalogue, ye go for men As hounds and greyhounds, mongrels, spaniels, curs, Shoughs, water-sugs, and demi-wolves, are cleped All by the name of dogs." (Act 3, Sc. 1.)

As Coriolanus is held up to our view as a pattern of noble bearing toward the people, so Richard II. condemns the courteous behavior of the future Henry IV. on his way into banishment. He says:

"Ourselves, and Bushy, Bagot here and Green Observed his courtship to the common people; How he did seem to dive into their hearts With humble and familiar courtesy; What reverence he did throw away on slaves; Wooing poor craftsmen with the craft of smiles And patient overbearing of his fortune, As 'twere to banish their effects with him. Off goes his bonnet to an oyster-wench; A brace of draymen did God speed him well And had the tribute of his supple knee, With 'Thanks, my countrymen, my loving friends.'" (Richard II., Act 1, Sc. 4.)

The King of France, in "All's Well that Ends Well," commends to Bertram the example of his late father in his relations with his inferiors:

"Who were below him He used as creatures of another place, And bowed his eminent top to their low ranks, Making them proud of his humility In their poor praise he humbled. Such a man Might be a copy to these younger times." (Act 1, Sc. 2.)

Shakespeare had no fondness for these "younger times," with their increasing suggestion of democracy. Despising the masses, he had no sympathy with the idea of improving their condition or increasing their power. He saw the signs of the times with foreboding, as did his hero, Hamlet:

"By the Lord, Horatio, these three years I have taken note of it; the age has grown so picked, that the toe of the peasant comes so near the heel of the courtier, he galls his kibe." There can easily be too much liberty, according to Shakespeare--"too much liberty, my Lucio, liberty" (Measure for Measure, Act 1, Sc. 3), but the idea of too much authority is foreign to him. Claudio, himself under arrest, sings its praises:

"Thus can the demi-god, Authority, Make us pay down for our offense by weight,-- The words of Heaven;--on whom it will, it will; On whom it will not, so; yet still 'tis just." (Ib.)

Ulysses, in "Troilus and Cressida" (Act 1, Sc. 3), delivers a long panegyric upon authority, rank, and degree, which may be taken as Shakespeare's confession of faith:

"Degree being vizarded, Th' unworthiest shews as fairly in the mask. The heavens themselves, the planets, and this center, Observe degree, priority, and place, Insisture, course, proportion, season, form, Office and custom, in all line of order; And therefore is the glorious planet, Sol, In noble eminence enthroned and sphered Amidst the other; whose med'cinable eye Corrects the ill aspects of planets evil, And posts, like the commandments of a king, Sans check, to good and bad. But when the planets, In evil mixture, to disorder wander, What plagues and what portents! what mutiny! What raging of the sea, shaking of the earth, Commotion of the winds, frights, changes, horrors, Divert and crack, rend and deracinate The unity and married calm of states Quite from their fixture! Oh, when degree is shaked, Which is the ladder of all high designs, The enterprise is sick. How could communities, Degrees in schools, and brotherhoods in cities, Peaceful commerce from dividable shores, The primogenity and due of birth, Prerogative of age, crowns, scepters, laurels, But by degree stand in authentic place? Take but degree away, untune the string, And hark, what discord follows! each thing meets In mere oppugnancy; the bounded waters Should lift their bosoms higher than the shores, And make a sop of all this solid globe; Strength should be lord of imbecility, And the rude son should strike his father dead; Force should be right; or, rather, right and wrong, (Between whose endless jar justice resides) Should lose their names, and so should justice too. Then everything includes itself in power. Power into will, will into appetite; And appetite, a universal wolf, So doubly seconded with will and power, Must make perforce an universal prey, And last eat up himself. Great Agamemnon, This chaos, when degree is suffocate, Follows the choking; And this neglect of degree it is, That by a pace goes backward, in a purpose It hath to climb. The General's disdained By him one step below; he by the next; That next by him beneath; so every step, Exampled by the first pace that is sick Of his superiors, grows to an envious fever Of pale and bloodless emulation; And 'tis this fever that keeps Troy on foot, Not her own sinews. To end a tale of length, Troy in our weakness stands, not in her strength."

There is no hint in this eloquent apostrophe of the difficulty of determining among men who shall be the sun and who the satellite, nor of the fact that the actual arrangements, in Shakespeare's time, at any rate, depended altogether upon that very force which Ulysses deprecates. In another scene in the same play the wily Ithacan again gives way to his passion for authority and eulogizes somewhat extravagantly the paternal, prying, omnipresent State:

"The providence that's in a watchful state Knows almost every grain of Plutus' gold, Finds bottom in th' incomprehensive deeps, Keeps place with thought, and almost, like the gods, Does thoughts unveil in their dumb cradles. There is a mystery (with which relation Durst never meddle) in the soul of state, Which hath an operation more divine Than breath or pen can give expressure to." (Act 3, Sc. 3.)

The State to which Ulysses refers is of course a monarchical State, and the idea of democracy is abhorrent to Shakespeare. Coriolanus expresses his opinion of it when he says to the people:

"What's the matter, That in these several places of the city You cry against the noble Senate, who, Under the gods, keep you in awe, which else Would feed on one another?" (Act 2, Sc. 1.)

The people should have no voice in the government--

"This double worship,-- Where one part does disdain with cause, the other Insult without all reason, where gentry, title, wisdom, Can not conclude, but by the yea and no Of general ignorance,--it must omit Real necessities, and give away the while To unstable slightness. Purpose so barred, it follows, Nothing is done to purpose; therefore, beseech you, You that will be less fearful than discreet, That love the fundamental part of state More than you doubt the change on't, that prefer A noble life before a long, and wish To jump a body with a dangerous physic That's sure of death without it, at once pluck out The multitudinous tongue; let them not lick The sweet which is their poison." (Ib. Act 3, Sc. 1.)

It is the nobility who should rule--

"It is a purposed thing and grows by plot To curb the will of the nobility; Suffer't and live with such as can not rule, Nor ever will be ruled." (Ib.)

Junius Brutus tries in vain to argue with him, but Coriolanus has no patience with him, a "triton of the minnows"; and the very fact that there should be tribunes appointed for the people disgusts him--

"Five tribunes to defend their vulgar wisdoms, Of their own choice; one's Junius Brutus, Sicinus Velutus, and I know not--'Sdeath! The rabble should have first unroofed the city, Ere so prevailed with me; it will in time Win upon power, and throw forth greater themes."

And again:

"The common file, a plague!--Tribunes for them!" (Act 1, Sc. 6.)

Shakespeare took his material for the drama of "Coriolanus" from Plutarch's "Lives," and it is significant that he selected from that list of worthies the most conspicuous adversary of the commonalty that Rome produced. He presents him to us as a hero, and, so far as he can, enlists our sympathy for him from beginning to end. When Menenius says of him:

"His nature is too noble for the world," (Act 3, Sc. 1.)

he is evidently but registering the verdict of the author. Plutarch's treatment of Coriolanus is far different. He exhibits his fine qualities, but he does not hesitate to speak of his "imperious temper and that savage manner which was too haughty for a republic." "Indeed," he adds, "there is no other advantage to be had from a liberal education equal to that of polishing and softening our nature by reason and discipline." He also tells us that Coriolanus indulged his "irascible passions on a supposition that they have something great and exalted in them," and that he wanted "a due mixture of gravity and mildness, which are the chief political virtues and the fruits of reason and education." "He never dreamed that such obstinacy is rather the effect of the weakness and effeminacy of a distempered mind, which breaks out in violent passions like so many tumors." Nor apparently did Shakespeare ever dream of it either, altho he had Plutarch's sage observations before him. It is a pity that the great dramatist did not select from Plutarch's works some hero who took the side of the people, some Agis or Cleomenes, or, better yet, one of the Gracchi. What a tragedy he might have based on the life of Tiberius, the friend of the people and the martyr in their cause! But the spirit which guided Schiller in the choice of William

Tell for a hero was a stranger to Shakespeare's heart, and its promptings would have met with no response there.

Even more striking is the treatment which the author of "Coriolanus" metes out to English history. All but two of his English historical dramas are devoted to the War of the Roses and the incidental struggle over the French crown. The motive of this prolonged strife--so attractive to Shakespeare--had much the same dignity which distinguishes the family intrigues of the Sublime Porte, and Shakespeare presents the history of his country as a mere pageant of warring royalties and their trains. When the people are permitted to appear, as they do in Cade's rebellion, to which Shakespeare has assigned the character of the rising under Wat Tyler, they are made the subject of burlesque. Two of the popular party speak as follows:

"John Holland. Well, I say, it was never merry world in England since gentlemen came up.

George Bevis. O miserable age! Virtue is not regarded in handicraftsmen.

John. The nobility think scorn to go in leather aprons."

When Jack Cade, alias Wat Tyler, comes on the scene, he shows himself to be a braggart and a fool. He says:

"Be brave then, for your captain is brave and vows reformation. There shall be in England seven half-penny loaves sold for a penny; the three-hooped pot shall have ten hoops, and I will make it a felony to drink small beer. All the realm shall be in common, and in Cheapside shall my palfrey go to grass. And when I am king asking I will be--

All. God save your majesty!

Cade. I thank you, good people--there shall be no money; all shall eat and drink on my score, and I will apparel them all in one livery, that they may agree like brothers and worship me their lord." (Henry VI., Part 2, Act 4, Sc. 2.)

The crowd wishes to kill the clerk of Chatham because he can read, write, and cast accounts. (Cade. "O monstrous!") Sir Humphrey Stafford calls them

"Rebellious hinds, the filth and scum of Kent, Marked for the gallows." (Ib.)

Clifford succeeds without much difficulty in turning the enmity of the mob against France, and Cade ejaculates disconsolately, "Was ever a feather so lightly blown to and fro as this multitude?" (Ib., Act 4, Sc. 8.) In the stage directions of this scene, Shakespeare shows his own opinion of the mob by writing, "Enter Cade and his rabblement." One looks in vain here as in the Roman plays for a suggestion that poor people sometimes suffer wrongfully from hunger and want, that they occasionally have just grievances, and that their efforts to present them, so far from being ludicrous, are the most serious parts of history, beside which the struttings of kings and courtiers sink into insignificance.

One of the popular songs in Tyler's rebellion was the familiar couplet:

"When Adam delved and Eve span, Who was then the gentleman?"

Shakespeare refers to it in "Hamlet," where the grave-diggers speak as follows:

"First Clown. Come, my spade. There is no ancient gentleman but gardners, ditchers and grave-makers; they hold up Adam's profession.

Second Clown. Was he a gentleman?

First Clown. He was the first that ever bore arms.

Second Clown. Why, he had none.

First Clown. What, art a heathen? How dost thou understand the Scripture? The Scripture says, Adam digged; could he dig without arms?" (Act 5, Sc. 1.)

That Shakespeare's caricature of Tyler's rebellion is a fair indication of his view of all popular risings appears from the remarks addressed by Westmoreland to the Archbishop of York in the Second Part of "Henry IV." (Act 4, Sc. 1). Says he:

"If that rebellion Came like itself, in base and abject routs, Led on by bloody youth, guarded with rags, And countenanced by boys and beggary; I say if damned commotion so appeared, In his true, native, and most proper shape, You, Reverend Father, and these noble lords Had not been here to dress the ugly form Of base and bloody insurrection With your fair honors."

The first and last of Shakespeare's English historical plays, "King John" and "Henry VIII.," lie beyond the limits of the civil wars, and each of them treats of a period momentous in the annals of English liberty, a fact which Shakespeare absolutely ignores. John as king had two great misfortunes--he suffered disgrace at the hands of his barons and of the pope. The first event, the wringing of Magna Charta from the king, Shakespeare passes over. A sense of national pride might have excused the omission of the latter humiliation, but no, it was a triumph of authority, and as such Shakespeare must record it for the edification of his hearers, and consequently we have the king presented on the stage as meekly receiving the crown from the papal legate (Act 5, Sc. 1). England was freed from the Roman yoke in the reign of Henry VIII., and in the drama of that name Shakespeare might have balanced the indignity forced upon King John, but now he is silent. Nothing must be said against authority, even against that of the pope, and the play culminates in the pomp and parade of the christening of the infant Elizabeth! Such is Shakespeare's conception of history! Who could guess from reading these English historical plays that throughout the period which they cover English freedom was growing, that justice and the rights of man were asserting themselves, while despotism was gradually curbed and limited? This is the one great glory of English history, exhibiting itself at Runnymede, reflected in Wyclif and John Ball and Wat Tyler, and shining dimly in the birth of a national church under the eighth Henry. As Shakespeare wrote, it was preparing for a new and conspicuous outburst. When he died, Oliver Cromwell was already seventeen years of age and John Hampden twenty-two.

The spirit of Hampden was preeminently the English spirit--the spirit which has given distinction to the Anglo-Saxon race--and he and Shakespeare were contemporaries, and yet of this spirit not a vestige is to be found in the English historical plays and no opportunities lost to obliterate or distort its manifestations. Only in Brutus and his fellow-conspirators--of all Shakespearian characters--do we find the least consideration for liberty, and even then he makes the common, and perhaps in his time the unavoidable, mistake of overlooking the genuinely democratic leanings of Julius Cæsar and the anti-popular character of the successful plot against him.

It has in all ages been a pastime of noble minds to try to depict a perfect state of society. Forty years before Shakespeare's birth, Sir Thomas More published his "Utopia" to the world. Bacon intended to do the same thing in the "New Atlantis," but never completed the work, while Sir Philip Sidney gives us his dream in his "Arcadia." Montaigne makes a similar essay, and we quote from Florio's translation, published in 1603, the following passage (Montaigne's "Essays," Book I, Chapter 30):

"It is a nation, would I answer Plato, that hath no kind of traffic, no knowledge of letters, no intelligence of numbers, no name of magistrate nor of political superiority; no use of service, of riches, or of poverty; no contracts, no succession, no dividences; no occupation, but idle; no respect of kindred, but common; no apparel, but natural; no manuring of lands; no use of wine, corn, or metal. The very words that import lying, falsehood, treason, dissimulation, covetousness, envy, detraction, and pardon were never heard among them."

We may readily infer that Shakespeare found little to sympathize with in this somewhat extravagant outline of a happy nation, but he goes out of his way to travesty it. In "The Tempest" he makes Gonzalo, the noblest character in the play, hold the following language to the inevitable king (Shakespeare can not imagine even a desert island without a king!):

"Had I plantation of this isle, my lord, I' th' commonwealth I would by contraries Execute all things; for no kind of traffic Would I admit; no name of magistrate; Letters should not be known; riches, poverty, And use of service, none; contract, succession, Bourn, bound of land, tilth, vineyard, none; No use of metal, corn or wine or oil; No occupation; all men idle,--all, And women too, but innocent and pure; No sovereignty, ...

Sebastian. Yet he would be king on't.

Antonia. The latter end of his commonwealth forgets the beginning.

Gonzalo. All things in common. Nature should produce Without sweat or endeavor; treason, felony, Sword, pike, knife, gun, or need of any engine, Would I not have; but Nature should bring forth Of its own kind, all foison, all abundance, To feed my innocent people.

Seb. No marrying 'mong his subjects?

Ant. None, man; all idle, whores, and knaves.

Gon. I would with such perfection govern, sir, To 'xcel the golden age.

Seb. 'Save his Majesty!

Ant. Long live Gonzalo!

Gon. And do you mark me, sir?

King. Pr'ythee, no more; thou dost talk nothing to me.

Gon. I do well believe your Highness; and did it to minister occasion to these gentlemen, who are of such sensible and nimble lungs that they always use to laugh at nothing.

Ant. 'Twas you we laughed at.

Gon. Who, in this kind of merry fooling, am nothing to you; so you may continue and laugh at nothing still." (Tempest, Act 2, Sc. 1.)

That all things are not for the best in the best of all possible worlds would seem to result from the wise remarks made by the fishermen who enliven the scene in "Pericles, Prince of Tyre." They compare landlords to whales who swallow up everything, and suggest that the land be purged of "these drones that rob the bee of her honey"; and

Pericles, so far from being shocked at such revolutionary and vulgar sentiments, is impressed by their weight, and speaks kindly of the humble philosophers, who in their turn are hospitable to the shipwrecked prince--all of which un-Shakespearian matter adds doubt to the authenticity of this drama (Act 2, Sc. 1).

However keen the insight of Shakespeare may have been into the hearts of his high-born characters, he had no conception of the unity of the human race. For him the prince and the peasant were not of the same blood.

"For princes are A model, which heaven makes like to itself,"

says King Simonides in "Pericles," and here at least we seem to see the hand of Shakespeare (Act 2, Sc. 2). The two princes, Guiderius and Arviragus, brought up secretly in a cave, show their royal origin (Cymbeline, Act 3, Sc. 3), and the servants who see Coriolanus in disguise are struck by his noble figure (Coriolanus, Act 4, Sc. 5). Bastards are villains as a matter of course, witness Edmund in "Lear" and John in "Much Ado about Nothing," and no degree of contempt is too high for a

"hedge-born swain That doth presume to boast of gentle blood." (Henry VI., Part 1, Act 4, Sc. 1.)

Courage is only to be expected in the noble-born. The Duke of York says:

"Let pale-faced fear keep with the mean-born man, And find no harbor in a royal heart." (Henry VI., Part 2, Act 3, Sc. 1.)

In so far as the lower classes had any relation to the upper classes, it was one, thought Shakespeare, of dependence and obligation. It was not the tiller of the soil who fed the lord of the manor, but rather the lord who supported the peasant. Does not the king have to lie awake and take thought for his subjects? Thus Henry V. complains that he can not sleep

"so soundly as the wretched slave, Who with a body filled and vacant mind, Gets him to rest, crammed with distressful bread, Never sees horrid night, the child of Hell, But like a lackey, from the rise to set, Sweats in the eye of Phoebus, and all night Sleeps in

Elysium.... The slave, a member of the country's peace, Enjoys it, but in gross brain little wots What watch the king keeps to maintain the peace, Whose hours the peasant best advantages." (Henry V., Act 4, Sc. 1.)

And these lines occur at the end of a passage in which the king laments the "ceremony" that oppresses him and confesses that but for it he would be "but a man." He makes this admission, however, in a moment of danger and depression. Henry IV. also invokes sleep (Part 2, Act 2, Sc. 1):

"O thou dull god! why liest thou with the vile In loathsome beds?"

But plain people have to watch at times, and the French sentinel finds occasion to speak in the same strain:

"Thus are poor servitors (When others sleep upon their quiet beds) Constrained to watch in darkness, rain, and cold." (Henry VI., Part 1, Act 2, Sc. 1.)

Henry VI. is also attracted by the peasant's lot:

"O God, methinks it were a happy life, To be no better than a homely swain.... ... The shepherd's homely curds, His cold thin drink out of his leather bottle, His wonted sleep under a fresh tree's shade, All which secure and sweetly he enjoys, As far beyond a prince's delicates." (Henry VI., Part 3, Act 2, Sc. 5.)

All of which is natural enough, but savors of cant in the mouths of men who fought long and hard to maintain themselves upon their thrones.

We have already shown by references to the contemporary drama that the plea of custom is not sufficient to explain Shakespeare's attitude to the lower classes, but if we widen our survey to the entire field of English letters in his day, we shall see that he was running counter to all the best traditions of our literature. From the time of Piers Plowman down, the peasant had stood high with the great writers of poetry and prose alike. Chaucer's famous circle of story-tellers at the Tabard Inn in Southwark was eminently democratic. With the knight and the friar were gathered together

"An haberdasher and a carpenter, A webbe, a deyer and tapiser,"

and the tales of the cook and the miller take rank with those of the squire and lawyer. The English Bible, too, was in Shakespeare's hands, and he must have been familiar with shepherd kings and fishermen-apostles. In the very year in which "Hamlet" first appeared, a work was published in Spain which was at once translated into English, a work as well known to-day as Shakespeare's own writings. If the peasantry was anywhere to be neglected and despised, where should it be rather than in proud, aristocratic Spain, and yet, to place beside Shakespeare's Bottoms and Slys, Cervantes has given us the admirable Sancho Panza, and has spread his loving humor in equal measure over servant and master. Are we to believe that the yeomen of England, who beat back the Armada, were inferior to the Spanish peasantry whom they overcame, or is it not rather true that the Spanish author had a deeper insight into his country's heart than was allotted to the English dramatist? Cervantes, the soldier and adventurer, rose above the prejudices of his class, while Shakespeare never lifted his eyes beyond the narrow horizon of the Court to which he catered. It was love that opened Cervantes's eye, and it is in all-embracing love that Shakespeare was deficient. As far as the common people were concerned, he never held the mirror up to nature.

But the book of all others which might have suggested to Shakespeare that there was more in the claims of the lower classes than was dreamt of in his philosophy was More's "Utopia," which in its English form was already a classic. More, the richest and most powerful man in England after the king, not only believed in the workingman, but knew that he suffered from unjust social conditions. He could never have represented the down-trodden followers of Cade-Tyler nor the hungry mob in "Coriolanus" with the utter lack of sympathy which Shakespeare manifests. "What justice is there in this," asks the great Lord Chancellor, whose character stood the test of death--"what justice is there in this, that a nobleman, a goldsmith, a banker, or any other man, that either does nothing at all or at best is employed in things that are of no use to the public, should live in great luxury and splendor upon what is so ill acquired; and a mean man, a carter, a smith, a plowman, that works harder even than the beasts themselves, and is employed on labors so necessary that no commonwealth could hold out a year without them, can only earn so poor a livelihood, and must lead so miserable a life, that the condition of the beasts is much better than theirs?"

How different from this is Shakespeare's conception of the place of the workingman in society! After a full and candid survey of his plays, Bottom, the weaver with the ass's head, remains his type of the artizan and the "mutable, rank-scented many," his type of the masses. Is it unfair to take the misshapen "servant-monster" Caliban as his last word on the subject?

"Prospero. We'll visit Caliban my slave who never Yields us kind answer.

Miranda. 'Tis a villain, sir, I do not love to look on.

Prospero. But as 'tis, We can not miss him! he does make our fire, Fetch in our wood, and serve in offices That profit us." (Tempest, Act 1, Sc. 2.)

To which I would fain reply in the words of Edward Carpenter:

"Who art thou ... With thy faint sneer for him who wins thee bread And him who clothes thee, and for him who toils Day-long and night-long dark in the earth for thee?"

LETTER FROM MR. G. BERNARD SHAW

(Extracts)

As you know, I have striven hard to open English eyes to the emptiness of Shakespeare's philosophy, to the superficiality and second-handedness of his morality, to his weakness and incoherence as a thinker, to his snobbery, his vulgar prejudices, his ignorance, his disqualifications of all sorts for the philosophic eminence claimed for him.... The preface to my "Three Plays for Puritans" contains a section headed "Better than Shakespeare?" which is, I think, the only utterance of mine on the subject to be found in a book.... There is at present in the press a new preface to an old novel of mine called "The Irrational Knot." In that preface I define the first order in Literature as consisting of those works in which the author, instead of accepting the current morality and religion ready-made without any question as to their validity, writes from an original moral standpoint of his own, thereby making his book an original contribution to morals, religion, and sociology, as well as to *belles letters*. I place Shakespeare with Dickens, Scott, Dumas père, etc., in the second order, because, tho they are enormously entertaining, their morality is ready-made; and I point out that the one play, "Hamlet," in which Shakespeare made an attempt to give as a hero one who was dissatisfied with the ready-made morality, is the one which has given the highest impression of his genius, altho Hamlet's revolt is unskillfully and inconclusively suggested and not worked out with any philosophic competence.[4]

May I suggest that you should be careful not to imply that Tolstoy's great Shakespearian heresy has no other support than mine. The preface of Nicholas Rowe to his edition of Shakespeare, and the various prefaces of Dr. Johnson contain, on Rowe's part, an apology for him as a writer with obvious and admitted shortcomings (very ridiculously ascribed by Rowe to his working by "a mere light of nature"), and, on Johnson's, a good deal of downright hard-hitting criticism. You should also look up the history of the Ireland forgeries, unless, as is very probable, Tolstoy has anticipated you in this. Among nineteenth-century poets Byron and William Morris saw clearly that Shakespeare was enormously overrated intellectually. A French book, which has been translated into English, has appeared within the last ten years, giving Napoleon's opinions of the drama. His insistence on the superiority of Corneille to Shakespeare on the ground of Corneille's power of grasping a political situation, and of seeing men in their relation to the state, is interesting.

Of course you know about Voltaire's criticisms, which are the more noteworthy because Voltaire began with an extravagant admiration for Shakespeare, and got more and more bitter against him as he grew older and less disposed to accept artistic merit as a cover for philosophic deficiencies.

Finally, I, for one, shall value Tolstoy's criticism all the more because it is criticism of a foreigner who can not possibly be enchanted by the mere word-music which makes Shakespeare so irresistible in England.[5] In Tolstoy's estimation, Shakespeare must fall or stand as a thinker, in which capacity I do not think he will stand a moment's examination from so tremendously keen a critic and religious realist. Unfortunately, the English worship their great artists quite indiscriminately and abjectly; so that is quite impossible to make them understand that Shakespeare's extraordinary literary power, his fun, his mimicry, and the endearing qualities that earned him the title of "the gentle Shakespeare"--all of which, whatever Tolstoy may say, are quite unquestionable facts--do not stand or fall with his absurd reputation as a thinker. Tolstoy will certainly treat that side of his reputation with the severity it deserves; and you will find that the English press will instantly announce that Tolstoy considers his own works greater than Shakespeare's (which in some respects they most certainly are, by the way), and that he has attempted to stigmatize our greatest poet as a liar, a thief, a forger, a murderer, an incendiary, a drunkard, a libertine, a fool, a madman, a coward, a vagabond, and even a man of questionable gentility. You must not be surprised or indignant at this: it is what is called "dramatic criticism" in England and America. Only a few of the best of our journalist-critics will say anything worth reading on the subject.

Yours faithfully, G. BERNARD SHAW.

FOOTNOTES:

[4] Besides the prefaces here referred to, Mr. G. Bernard Shaw has at various times written other articles on the subject.--(V. T.)

[5] It should be borne in mind that this letter was written before Mr. G. B. Shaw had seen the essay in question, by Tolstoy, now published in this volume.--(V. T.)

"No one will peruse a page without laying down the book a better and a wiser man."--*Dundee Courier.*

Tolstoy's Essays and Letters

By LEO TOLSTOY

Translated by AYLMER MAUDE

This work contains twenty-six essays and letters (many published for the first time) belonging to the last fifteen years of Tolstoy's career, the period in which he has devoted himself exclusively to humanitarian labors. Therefore each has a definite altruistic purpose. In the letters in particular we have, in the words of the translator, "Tolstoy's opinions in application to certain definite conditions. They thus help to bridge the gulf between theory and practise."

HIGHLY COMMENDED

"The subjects are varied, and present Tolstoy's well-known views in his always forceful manner."--*The Outlook.*

"It contains the Russian philosopher and philanthropist's best thought, and furnishes considerable insight into his wonderful personality."--*The Mirror, St. Louis.*

"For those who wish to be well instructed in Tolstoyana this handy little book will be invaluable."--*Brooklyn Eagle.*

"These essays form an admirable introduction to Tolstoy's philosophy."--*Western Daily Mercury*, Plymouth, Eng.

12mo, Cloth, 372 pp. Price, $1.00, post-paid

FUNK & WAGNALLS COMPANY, Publishers NEW YORK and LONDON

* * * * *

Tolstoy's Plays

Also Annotated List of Works

This volume, a new translation by Louise and Aylmer Maude, contains Tolstoy's three great plays, together with the Russian folk-tale of which one of them is the dramatized version. It also includes a complete annotated and chronological list of Tolstoy's works of special helpfulness to all readers and students of the great Russian writer.

LIST OF THE PLAYS

=The Power of Darkness=; or, If a Claw is Caught the Bird is Lost--A drama in five acts.

=The First Distiller=--A comedy in six acts.

=Fruits of Culture=--A comedy in four acts.

INCLUDING ALSO

=The Imp and the Crust=--This is a Russian folk-tale, of which "The First Distiller" is the dramatized version.

=Their High Literary and Dramatic Value=

To their literary merit Tolstoy's plays add the quality of being excellent acting dramas, as their success both in Russia and elsewhere has abundantly shown. Mr. Laurence Irving lately wrote: "I suppose England is the only country in Europe where 'The Power of Darkness' has not been acted. It ought to be done. It is a stupendous tragedy; the effect on the stage is unparalleled."

=Their Wide Range of Sentiment=

"Between Tolstoy's two great plays," says the translator, "'The Power of Darkness' and 'The Fruits of Culture,' the contrast is very striking. The first is intensely moral, terrible in its earnestness and force.... Very different is 'Fruits of Culture,' a play brimful of laughter and merriment."

Handsomely printed on deckle-edge paper, gilt-top, half-tone frontispiece, showing Anisya and Nikita in "The Power of Darkness," cover design in gold, extra-quality ribbed olive cloth, 250 + xii pages. Price $1.50, post-paid.

FUNK & WAGNALLS COMPANY New York PUBLISHERS London

* * * * *

A CLEAR AND HOPEFUL EXPOSITION OF TOLSTOY'S TEACHINGS

"Students of the master will find this little book indispensable."--*San Francisco News-Letter.*

Tolstoy and His Problems

Essays by AYLMER MAUDE

Each essay in this volume expresses, in one form or other, Tolstoy's views of life; and the main object of the book is not to praise his views, but to explain them. Being the only Englishman who in recent years has had the advantage of intimate personal intercourse, continued over a period of some years, with Tolstoy, Mr. Maude is well qualified for his present work.

CONTENTS

Biography of Tolstoy | Introduction to "The Slavery Tolstoy's Teachings | of Our Times" An Introduction to "What | The Tsar's Coronation Is Art?" | Right and Wrong How "Resurrection" Was | War and Patriotism Written | Talks With Tolstoy

"Any one who takes up this delightful series of essays will not willingly lay it down without at least the determination to finish it."--*British Friend.*

"Mr. Maude's long and intimate acquaintance with Tolstoy enables him to speak with knowledge probably not possessed by any other Englishman."--*Morning Post.*

12mo, Cloth, 220 pages. Price, $1.00

FUNK & WAGNALLS COMPANY, Publishers NEW YORK and LONDON

* * * * *

Sevastopol

AND OTHER MILITARY TALES

By LEO TOLSTOY

A new translation by Louise and Aylmer Maude, specially approved by the author. This book relates the author's own experiences, sensations, and reflections during the most noted siege of modern history. The translation has been authorized by Count

Tolstoy, who has specially commended it for its accuracy, simplicity, and directness.

"No other modern book approaches 'Sevastopol' in the completeness and directness with which it unveils the realities of war. There are picturesque glimpses in Mr. Kipling's vulgar stories of fighting. But the strongest meat Mr. Kipling can provide is milk for babes beside Count Tolstoy's seemingly casual sketches, which yet comprehend with merciless amplitude the whole atmosphere of war."--*The Morning Leader*, London.

What Count Tolstoy Says of the Translators and Translation

"Better translators, both for knowledge of the two languages and for penetration into the very meaning of the matter translated, could not be invented." Of their translation of Sevastopol, Tolstoy also says: "I think I already wrote you how unusually the first volume of your edition pleases me. All in it is excellent: the edition and the remarks, and chiefly the translation, and yet more the conscientiousness with which all this has been done."

Handsomely printed on deckle-edge paper, gilt top, photogravure portrait of Tolstoy from a daguerreotype taken in 1855, map of Sevastopol; cover design in gold, extra-quality ribbed olive cloth, 325 + xlviii. pp. $1.50.

(*This book is not for sale by us in Great Britain.*)

FUNK & WAGNALLS COMPANY, Publishers NEW YORK and LONDON

* * * * *

Three New Stories by Count Leo Tolstoy, Written for the Benefit of the Kishinef Sufferers. Publisher's and Author's Profits are to go to the Kishinef Relief Fund

ESARHADDON

King of Assyria, and Other Stories

By COUNT LEO TOLSTOY

Translated by Louise and Aylmer Maude, with an Introduction Containing Letters by Tolstoy

=Esarhaddon, King of Assyria.= An allegorical story with an Oriental setting, telling how a cruel king was made to feel and understand the sufferings of one of his captives, and to repent his own cruelty.

=Work, Death, and Sickness.= A legend accredited to the South American Indians, showing the three means God took to make men more kind and brotherly toward each other.

=Three Questions.= A quaint folk-lore tale answering the three questions of life: "What is the Best Time?" "Who Are the Most Important Persons?" "What Thing Should be Done First?"

OPINION OF THE PRESS

St. Louis Globe-Democrat: "Count Tolstoy is a man so sure of his message and so clear about it that he always finds something worth while to say.... There is a quality in the little tales published under the title 'Esarhaddon' which is quickly suggestive of certain Biblical narratives. There is one called 'Three Questions,' which contains, in half a dozen pages, an entire philosophy of life, and it is presented in such apt pictures and ideas that its meaning is not to be overlooked. It would be hard to suggest anything that could be read in five minutes that would impart so much to think about. 'Esarhaddon,' the sketch from which the volume takes its name, is of the same character, and the third tale, 'Work, Death, and Sickness,' is full of very fine thought. There is, perhaps, no writer working to-day whose mind is centered on broader and better things than the Russian master, and the present offering shows him at his very best."

"Hour-Glass Stories." Dainty 12mo, Cloth, Frontispiece, Ornamental Cover, 40 cents, Postpaid

FUNK & WAGNALLS COMPANY, Publishers NEW YORK and LONDON

* * * * *

What Is Art?

Translated from the Original Manuscript, with an Introduction by AYLMER MAUDE

Art is a human activity, declares Tolstoy. The object of this activity is to transmit to others feelings the artist has experienced. By certain external signs--movements, lines, colors, sounds or arrangements of words--an artist infects other people so that they share his feelings; thus, "art is a means of union among men, joining them together in the same feeling." Without adequate expression there is no art, for there is no infection, no transference to others of the author's feeling. The test of art is infection. If an author has moved you so that you feel as he felt, if you are so united to him in feeling that it seems to you that he has expressed just what you have long wished to express, the work that has so infected you is a work of art.

A POWERFUL WORK FULL OF GENIUS AND ORIGINALITY

"The powerful personality of the author, the startling originality of his views, grip the reader and carry him, though his deepest convictions be outraged, protesting through the book."--*Pall Mall Gazette.*

"The discussion is bound to shake the whole world to its very center, and to result in a considerable readjustment of theories."--*Pittsburg Times.*

"It is the ablest and most scholarly writing of a great thinker."--*Chicago Inter Ocean.*

"No recent book on the subject is so novel, so readable, or so questionable."--*New York Times Saturday Review.*

Small 12mo, Cloth, 268 pp. 80 cts., post-paid

FUNK & WAGNALLS COMPANY, Publishers NEW YORK and LONDON

Made in United States
Orlando, FL
05 December 2023